# 'DOMESTIC VIOLENCE ACT 2005' - SUPREME COURT'S LEADING CASE LAWS

## CASE NOTES- FACTS- FINDINGS OF APEX COURT JUDGES & CITATIONS

JAYPRAKASH BANSILAL SOMANI

All the Past & Present Judges of the Supreme Court of India.

Salute to their wisdom.

Salute to their interpretation of Law.

Salute to their elaborative judgement writing.

Supreme Court Of India

# Contents

# Contents

# Preface

Dear Learned Advocates ofTrial Court, High court and Supreme Court, Corporate and Individuals.

I am very delighted to provide you a book on'DOMESTIC VIOLENCE ACT 2005'- SUPREME COURT'S LATEST LEADING CASE LAWs

In this book you will get...

1. Name of the Case i. e. Cause title

2.Relevant Sections discussed in the case

3. Hon'ble Judges/Coram of the case

4.Number of PDF Pages in Original Judgement of the case

5. All available Citations of the case

6. Case Note with appeal allowed/ dismissed or disposed off

7. Facts of the case

8. Hon'ble Apex Court's findings, while dismissing/allowing or disposing the appeal

9. Ratio Decidendi if any.

My special thanks to Manupatra, because of their web portal I can compile this book in well manner. I am also thankful to Notion Press to support me to publish & market this book throughout the Country. Thanks to my Juniors, Advocate Colleagues & Insolvency Professional Colleagues to support me in this venture.

**Adv. Manoj Kumar Chowdhary & Miss. Pooja Rai** has helped me a lot to compile this book. I hope this book will add some value addition in the wealth of your legal knowledge. Your positive feedbacks will boost me to compile/ write further books & negative feedbacks will improve my skills. Kindly send your valuable feedbacks by email.

Thanks with Regards,

**Jayprakash B. Somani**

Advocate, Supreme Court of India

**Email:** jaysomani64@gmail.com

**Web Site:**www.jayprakashsomani.com

**Call:** 9322188701, 8459194576

# Acknowledgements

**Printed & Published by**
**Notion Press**
No. 8, 3rd Cross Street,
CIT Colony, Mylapore,
Chennai, Tamil Nadu- 600004
**Managed by**
**Jayprakash Somani Advocates & Solicitors**
**Law Firm for Supreme Court of India**
**Delhi Office**
B- 851, 1st Floor, Shivaji Marg, New Ashok Nagar, Delhi 110096.
Call: 9322188701, 8459194576
**Supreme Court Chamber**
312, 3rd Floor, M. C. Setalvad Block, In front of 'D' Gate, Bhagwan Das
Road, Supreme Court of India, New Delhi 110001
Contact: 8459194576, 9811011747
www.jayprakashsomani.com
**Download our app** to get access to our Free Videos, Free Bare Acts,
Free Study Material in Legal as well as International Business Regime.
**Android App Link** ;-https://clpandrea.page.link/cmSm
**Ios APp Link** :-https://apps.apple.com/us/app/classplus/id1324522260
**Login with org code** ;- (qywzji)
**Web Link** ;-https://qywzji.courses.store/
**Opportunity for Lawyers/ Social Workers** to get Supreme Court Law
Firm JSAS's authorised centre at District Level.
Kindly Message or Call to: 9322188701.
**Books are available online in India**
**1.Notion Press:**https://notionpress.com/author/jayprakash_somani
**2.Amazon:**https://www.amazon.in/s?k=jayprakash+somani
**3.Flipkart:**https://www.flipkart.com/search?q=Jayprakash%20Somani
**Books are available online at International Market**
**4. Amazon International:** https://www.amazon.com/
s?k=jayprakash+somani
**5. Amazon United Kingdom:** https://www.amazon.co.uk/
s?k=jayprakash+somani

**6. E-Books/Kindle edition at National & International Level:**
https://www.amazon.in/s?k=jaypraksh+somani

# CHAPTER ONE

# Prabha Tyagi vs. Kamlesh Devi (12.05.2022 - SC) : MANU/SC/0631/2022

**Relative Section:**

Bengal Finance Sales Tax Act, 1941 - Section 5(2); Bengal Sales Tax Rules - Rule 27A; Bombay Tenancy and Agricultural Lands Act, 1948; Code of Civil Procedure, 1908 (CPC); Code of Criminal Procedure, 1973 (CrPC) - Section 482; Constitution of India - Article 31B; Hindu Marriage Act, 1955; Maharashtra Agricultural Lands (Ceiling on Holdings) Act, 1961; Protection Of Women From Domestic Violence Act, 2005 - Section 1(d), Protection Of Women From Domestic Violence Act, 2005 - Section 2, Protection Of Women From Domestic Violence Act, 2005 - Section 2(a), Protection Of Women From Domestic Violence Act, 2005 - Section 2(f), Protection Of Women From Domestic Violence Act, 2005 - Section 2(s), Protection Of Women From Domestic Violence Act, 2005 - Section 3, Protection Of Women From Domestic Violence Act, 2005 - Section 8(1), Protection Of Women From Domestic Violence Act, 2005 - Section 8(2), Protection Of Women From Domestic Violence Act, 2005 - Section 9, Protection Of Women From Domestic Violence Act, 2005 - Section 9(1), Protection Of Women From Domestic Violence Act, 2005 - Section 10, Protection Of Women From Domestic Violence Act, 2005 - Section 10(1), Protection Of Women From Domestic Violence Act, 2005 - Section 12, Protection Of Women From Domestic Violence Act, 2005 - Section 12(1), Protection Of Women From Domestic Violence Act, 2005 - Section 17, Protection Of Women From Domestic Violence Act, 2005 - Section 17(1), Protection Of Women From Domestic Violence Act, 2005 - Section 17(2), Protection

Of Women From Domestic Violence Act, 2005 - Section 18, Protection Of Women From Domestic Violence Act, 2005 - Section 19, Protection Of Women From Domestic Violence Act, 2005 - Section 20, Protection Of Women From Domestic Violence Act, 2005 - Section 21, Protection Of Women From Domestic Violence Act, 2005 - Section 22; Protection Of Women From Domestic Violence Rules, 2006 - Rule 5, Protection Of Women From Domestic Violence Rules, 2006 - Rule 6; Special Marriage Act; Tamil Nadu Buildings (lease And Rent Control) Act, 1960 - Section 10(2); Trade Marks Act, 1940 - Section 6

**Hon'bleJudges/Coram:** M.R. Shah and B.V. Nagarathna, JJ.

**Equivalent Citation:** AIR2022SC2331, 2022 (2) ALD(Crl.) 891 (SC), 2022 (2) ALT (Crl.) 315 (A.P.), 2022(4)CivilCC(S.C.), 2022(3)CriminalCC1, II(2022)DMC308SC, 2022 (3) Him. LR. 198, 2022(2)HLR625, 2022/INSC/563, 2023(1)J.L.J.R.280, 2023(1)JKJ14[SC], 2022 (2) MWN (CR.) 17, 2022(3)N.C.C.474, 2023 (1)PLJR252, 2022(3)RCR(Criminal)9, 2022(2)RLW1679(SC), (2022)8SCC90, 2022(3)UC1505

**NumberofPagesintheOriginalJudgment:** 36

**Case Reference:**

Satish Chander Ahuja v. Sneha Ahuja MANU/SC/0767/2020; Juveria Abdul Majid Patni v. Atif Iqbal Mansoori MANU/SC/0861/2014; V.D. Bhanot v. Savita Bhanot MANU/SC/0115/2012; Krishna Bhatacharjee v. Sarathi Choudhury and Ors. MANU/SC/1330/2015; Saraswathy v. Babu MANU/SC/1193/2013; Jeet Singh and Ors. v. State of U.P. and Ors. MANU/SC/0436/1993; Rashmi Kumar v. Mahesh Kumar Bhada MANU/SC/1052/1997; Ajay Kumar v. Lata and Ors. MANU/SC/0651/2019; S.R. Batra and Ors. v. Taruna Batra MANU/SC/0007/2007; Harbhajan Singh v. Press Council of India and Ors. MANU/SC/0181/2002; D. Velusamy v. D. Patchaiammal MANU/SC/0872/2010; Indra Sarma v. V.K.V. Sarma MANU/SC/1230/2013; Nayanakumar v. The State of Karnataka and Anr. MANU/KA/0836/2009; Shambhu Prasad Singh v. Manjari MANU/DE/2152/2012; Ravi Dutta v. Kiran Dutta & Anr. MANU/DE/0419/2014; Ishverlal Thakorelal Almaula v. Motibhai Nagjibhai MANU/SC/0328/1965; Kaviraj Pandit Durga Dutt Sharma v. Navaratna Pharmaceutical Laboratories MANU/SC/0197/1964; Kedarnath Jute Manufacturing Co. v. Commercial Tax Officer, Calcutta and Ors. MANU/SC/0290/1965; Dattatraya Govind Mahajan and Ors. v. State of Maharashtra and Ors. MANU/SC/0381/1977; S. Sundaram Pillai and Ors. v. `R. Pattabiraman and

Ors. MANU/SC/0387/1985; M. Pentiah and Ors. v. Muddala Veeramallappa and Ors. MANU/SC/0263/1960; Superintendent and Remembrancer of Legal Affairs to Government of West Bengal v. Abani Maity MANU/SC/0524/1979; Smt. Bharati Naik v. Shri Ravi Ramnath Halarnkar and Anr.; Vandhana v. T. Srikanth and Krishnamachari; Abhiram Gogoi v. Rashmi Rekha Gogoi MANU/GH/0388/2011 : (2011) 4 Gauhati Law Reports 276; Md. Basit v. State of Assam and Ors. MANU/GH/0750/2011 : (2012) 1 Gauhati Law Reports 747; Rahul Soorma v. State of Himachal Pradesh; A. Vidya Sagar v. State of Andhra Pradesh; Ravi Kumar Bajpai v. Renu Awasthi Bajpai MANU/MP/0966/2015 : ILR (2016) MP 302; Rakesh Choudhary v. Vandana Choudhary; Vijay Maruti Gaikwad v. Savita Vijay Gaikward MANU/MH/4969/2017 : 2018 (1) HLR 295; Suraj Sharma v. Bharti Sharma; Rama Singh v. Maya Singh MANU/MP/1854/2012 : (2012) 4 MPLJ 612

**Case Note:**

Criminal - Domestic Violence - Complaint alleging domestic violence by aggrieved person - Section 12 of the Protection of Women from Domestic Violence Act, 2005 (DV Act) - Complaint allowed by Trial Court - First Appellate Court set aside the judgment - High Court in subsequent appeal affirmed the finding of First Appellate Court - High Court held that since complaint not accompanied by report statutory conditions not satisfied - Further aggrieved person resided separately from Respondents since date of her marriage - Hence the present appeal by aggrieved person - Whether the consideration of Domestic Incident Report mandatory before initiating the proceedings under DV Act? - Whether it is mandatory for the aggrieved person to reside with those persons against whom allegations levelled at the point of commission of violence? - Whether there should be a subsisting domestic relationship between the aggrieved person and the person against whom the relief is claimed?

**Facts:**

The aggrieved person (Appellant) filed complaint alleging domestic violence against her in-laws she suffered after the demise of her husband. As alleged she was denied of her stridhanaand also her rights in her deceased husbands' estate. The application filed by aggrieved person was partly allowed and Respondents were directed to pay monetary compensation for insulting and maligning the aggrieved person, besides making available articles of Stridhana. In the appeal preferred by Respondent No. 1, (mother-in-law of the aggrieved person), judgment of the Trial Court was set aside. Thereafter High Court in the impugned judgment held that aggrieved person had only filed an application alleging domestic violence and since the same was not accompanied by a report, the conditions of Section 12(1) of the D.V. Act were not satisfied. Further, the aggrieved person was residing separately from the Respondents from the day of her marriage and there was no domestic relationship between the aggrieved person and the Respondents, therefore, no relief could be granted under the provisions of the D.V. Act. Hence the present appeal by aggrieved person.

**Held, while allowing the Appeal:**

Section 12 of the D.V. Act states that an aggrieved person or a Protection Officer or any other person on behalf of the aggrieved person may present an application to the Magistrate seeking one or more reliefs under the D.V. Act. [22]

While the object and purpose of the D.V. Act is to protect a woman from domestic violence, the salutary object of Sub-section (1) of Section 17 is to confer a right on every woman in a domestic relationship to have the right to reside in a shared household. [27]

The D.V. Act is a piece of Civil Code which is applicable to every woman in India irrespective of her religious affiliation and/or social background for a more effective protection of her rights guaranteed under the Constitution and in order to protect women victims of domestic violence occurring in a domestic relationship. Therefore, the expression 'joint family' cannot mean as understood in Hindu Law. Thus, the expression 'family members living together as a joint family', means the members living jointly as a family. In such an interpretation, even a girl child/children who is/are cared for as foster children also have a right to live in a shared household and are conferred with the right Under Sub-section (1) of Section 17 of the D.V. Act. When such a girl child or woman becomes an aggrieved person, the protection of Sub-section (2) of Section 17 comes into play.[36]

It is not mandatory for the aggrieved person to have actually lived or resided with those persons against whom the allegations have been levelled at the time of seeking relief. If a woman has the right to reside in a shared household, she can accordingly enforce her right under Section 17(1) of the D.V. Act. If a woman becomes an aggrieved person or victim of domestic violence, she can seek relief under the provisions of the D.V. Act including her right to live or reside in the shared household under Section 17 read with Section 19 of the D.V. Act.[40]

Hence, the Appellant herein had the right to live in a shared household i.e., her matrimonial home and being a victim of domestic violence could enforce her right to live or reside in the shared household under the provisions of the D.V. Act and to seek any other appropriate relief provided under the D.V. Act. This is irrespective of whether she actually lived in the shared household.[41]

Even though as on the date of filing of the application before the Magistrate Under Section 12 of the D.V. Act the Appellant was not actually living in the shared household; she nevertheless lived in a domestic relationship with her husband and further had the right to reside in a shared household as a daughter-in-law. The Appellant-aggrieved person had to leave the shared household on account of harassment and mental torture given to her by Respondent - mother-in-law and her family. She had to leave the same and fend for herself. Thus, as an aggrieved person, the Appellant could not have been excluded from the shared household as there was no valid reason to do so. As the Appellant had a right to reside in the shared household as she was in a domestic relationship with her husband till he died in the accident and had lived together with him therefore she also had a right to reside in the shared household despite the death of her husband in a road accident. The aggrieved person continued to have a subsisting domestic relationship owing to her marriage and she being the daughter-in-law had the right to reside in the shared household.[44]

An aggrieved person on her own or any other person on behalf of the aggrieved person may present an application to the Magistrate seeking one or more reliefs under the D.V. Act but the proviso states that when a Domestic Incident Reported is received by the Magistrate from the Protection Officer or the service provider, in such a case, the same shall be taken into consideration. Therefore, when an aggrieved person files an application by herself or with the assistance of an advocate and not with the assistance of the Protection Officer or a service provider, in such a case, the role of the Protection Officer or a service provider is not envisaged. Although, the expression 'shall' is used in the proviso, it is restricted to only those cases where a Protection Officer files any Domestic Incident Report or, as the case may be, the service provider files such a report. When a Domestic Incident Report is filed by a Protection Officer or a service provider, in such a case the Magistrate has to take into consideration the said report received by him. But if such a report has not been filed on behalf of the aggrieved person then he is not bound to consider any such report.

Therefore, the expression 'shall' has to be read in the context of a Domestic Incident Report received by a Magistrate from the Protection Officer or the service provider as the case may be in which case, it is mandatory for the Magistrate to consider the report. But, if no such report is received by the Magistrate then the Magistrate is naturally not to consider any such Domestic Incident Report before passing any order on the application. [47]

High Court was not right in holding that the application filed by the Appellant herein was not accompanied by a Domestic Incident Report and therefore under the proviso to Sub-section (1) of Section 12 of the D.V. Act, the Magistrate had no authority to issue orders and directions in favour of the Appellant.[48]

The three questions raised in this appeal are answered as under: (i) Section 12 does not make it mandatory for a Magistrate to consider a Domestic Incident Report filed by a Protection Officer or service provider before passing any order under the D.V. Act. It is clarified that even in the absence of a Domestic Incident Report, a Magistrate is empowered to pass both ex parte or interim as well as a final order under the provisions of the D.V. Act.; (ii) It is not mandatory for the aggrieved person, when she is related by consanguinity, marriage or through a relationship in the nature of marriage, adoption or are family members living together as a joint family, to actually reside with those persons against whom the allegations have been levelled at the time of commission of domestic violence. If a woman has the right to reside in the shared household Under Section 17 of the D.V. Act and such a woman becomes an aggrieved person or victim of domestic violence, she can seek reliefs under the provisions of D.V. Act including enforcement of her right to live in a shared household; (iii) There should be a subsisting domestic relationship between the aggrieved person and the person against whom the relief is claimed vis-Ã-vis allegation of domestic violence. However, it is not necessary that at the time of filing of an application by an aggrieved person, the domestic relationship should be subsisting. [52]

The appeal is allowed in the aforesaid terms.[54]

Disposition: Appeal Allowed

# The State of Maharashtra vs. 63 Moons Technologies Ltd. (22.04.2022 - SC) : MANU/SC/0534/2022

**Relative Section:**

Code of Civil Procedure, 1908 (CPC) - Order 37; Andhra Pradesh Protection of Depositors of Financial Establishments Act, 1999; Banking Regulation Act, 1949 - Section 5, Banking Regulation Act, 1949 - Section 5(c); Chit Funds Act, 1982 - Section 2; Code of Criminal Procedure, 1973 (CrPC) - Section 173; Companies Act, 1956 - Section 209A, Companies Act, 1956 - Section 396, Companies Act, 1956 - Section 396(3); Constitution of India - Article 14, Constitution of India - Article 19, Constitution of India - Article 19(1), Constitution of India - Article 21, Constitution of India - Article 32, Constitution of India - Article 226, Constitution of India - Article 300A; Forward Contracts (regulation) Act, 1952 - Section 27; General Clauses Act 1897 - Section 3(42); Goa Protection of Interests of Depositors (in financial Establishments) Act, 1999; Himachal Pradesh [Protection of interests of depositors (in Financial Establishments) Act, 1999; Indian Penal Code, 1860 (IPC) - Section 120B, Indian Penal Code, 1860 (IPC) - Section 409, Indian Penal Code, 1860 (IPC) - Section 465, Indian Penal Code, 1860 (IPC) - Section 467, Indian Penal Code, 1860 (IPC) - Section 468, Indian Penal Code, 1860 (IPC) - Section 471, Indian Penal Code, 1860 (IPC) - Section 474, Indian Penal Code, 1860 (IPC) - Section 477A, Indian Penal Code, 1860 (IPC) - Section 477(4); Industrial Development Bank Of India Act, 1964 - Section 6A; Kerala Protection of

Interests of Depositors in Financial Establishment Act, 2013; Maharashtra Protection Of Interest Of Depositors (in Financial Establishments) Act, 1999 - Section 2, Maharashtra Protection Of Interest Of Depositors (in Financial Establishments) Act, 1999 - Section 2(c), Maharashtra Protection Of Interest Of Depositors (in Financial Establishments) Act, 1999 - Section 2(d), Maharashtra Protection Of Interest Of Depositors (in Financial Establishments) Act, 1999 - Section 3, Maharashtra Protection Of Interest Of Depositors (in Financial Establishments) Act, 1999 - Section 4, Maharashtra Protection Of Interest Of Depositors (in Financial Establishments) Act, 1999 - Section 4(1), Maharashtra Protection Of Interest Of Depositors (in Financial Establishments) Act, 1999 - Section 4(2), Maharashtra Protection Of Interest Of Depositors (in Financial Establishments) Act, 1999 - Section 5, Maharashtra Protection Of Interest Of Depositors (in Financial Establishments) Act, 1999 - Section 6, Maharashtra Protection Of Interest Of Depositors (in Financial Establishments) Act, 1999 - Section 7, Maharashtra Protection Of Interest Of Depositors (in Financial Establishments) Act, 1999 - Section 8, Maharashtra Protection Of Interest Of Depositors (in Financial Establishments) Act, 1999 - Section 10, Maharashtra Protection Of Interest Of Depositors (in Financial Establishments) Act, 1999 - Section 11; Odisha Protection of Interests of Depositors (in Financial Establishments) Act, 2011; Pondicherry Protection of Interests of Depositors in Financial Establishments Act, 2004; Protection Of Women From Domestic Violence Act, 2005 - Section 2(f); Securities and Exchange Board of India Act, 1992; Sikkim Protection of interests of Depositors (in Financial Establishments) Act, 2000; Tamil Nadu Protection Of Interests Of Depositors (in Financial Establishments) Act, 1997 - Section 2(2); Telangana Protection of Depositors of Financial Establishments Act, 1999

**Hon'bleJudges/Coram:** Dr. D.Y. Chandrachud, Surya Kant and Bela M. Trivedi, JJ.

**Equivalent Citation:**2022(4)ALLMR352, 2022(3)BomCR716, 2022/INSC/465, (2022)9SCC457, [2022] 173SCL53(SC)

**NumberofPagesintheOriginalJudgment: 46**

**Case Reference:**

63 Moons Technologies Ltd. and Ors. v. Union of India (UOI) and Ors. MANU/SC/0629/2019; New Horizon Sugar Mills Ltd. v. Govt. of Pondicherry MANU/SC/0796/2012; K.K. Baskaran v. State rep. by its Secretary, Tamil Nadu and Ors. MANU/SC/0181/2011; State and Ors. v.

K.S. Palanichamy and Ors. MANU/SC/0631/2017; P.G.F. Limited and Ors. v. Union of India (UOI) and Ors. MANU/SC/0247/2013; Mohinder Singh Gill and Ors. v. The Chief Election Commissioner, New Delhi and Ors. MANU/SC/0209/1977; Indra Sarma v. V.K.V. Sarma MANU/SC/1230/2013; Delhi Cloth & General Mills Co. Ltd. and Ors. v. Union of India (UOI) and Ors. MANU/SC/0377/1983; Shri Vijay C. Puljal v. State of Maharashtra and Ors. MANU/MH/0568/2005; Soma Suresh Kumar v. Government of Andhra Pradesh and Ors. MANU/SC/0924/2013; Karnataka Power Transmission Corpn. and Ors. v. Ashok Iron Works Pvt. Ltd. and Ors. MANU/SC/0158/2009; Ramanlal Bhailal Patel and Ors. v. State of Gujarat MANU/SC/7119/2008; K.K. Bhaskaran v. State; Sonal Hemant Joshi v. State of Maharashtra MANU/SC/1659/2011 : (2012) 10 SCC 601; State of Maharashtra v. Vijay C. Puljal MANU/SC/1658/2011 : (2012) 10 SCC 599

**Case Note:**

Capital Market - Exemption of forward contracts - Attachment of Property - Sections 2(d), 4 of the Maharashtra Protection of Interest of Depositors (in Financial Establishments) Act 1999 (MPID Act) - Section 27 of the Forward Contracts (Regulation) Act 1952 - Notifications issued directing attachment of properties quashed vide impugned judgment - Hence the present appeal - Whether National Spot Exchange Limited (NSEL) a financial establishment for the purpose of the MPID Act?

**Facts:**

The present appeal arose against the impugned judgment quashing certain notifications attaching the property of the Respondent under Section 4 of the MPID Act. The Respondent holds 99.99% of the shareholding of National Spot Exchange Limited (NSEL). At the core of the dispute is whether NSEL is a 'financial establishment' within the meaning of Section 2(d) of the MPID Act.The Union of India had issued a notification under Section 27 of the Forward Contracts (Regulation) Act 1952 exempting forward contacts of one-day duration for sale and purchase of commodities traded on NSEL from the application of the provisions of the enactment. NSEL started operating as an exchange for spot trading in commodities. NSEL launched contracts for buying and selling of commodities on its trading platform with different settlement periods. The Department of Consumer Affairs (DCA) issued a show cause notice to NSEL on why action should not be taken against it for permitting transactions in violation of the exemption notification. Subsequently Central Government withdrew the exemption granted. The Forward

Markets Commission recommended to DCA that steps be taken to ascertain the quantity and quality of commodities at accredited warehouses, the financial status of buyers and trading members, and that liability be fixed on the promoters of NSEL. The Union of India ordered inspection of accounts and cases were against the directors and key management personnel.NSEL filed a writ petition challenging the invocation of the MPID Act on the ground that exchange is not a 'financial establishment' under the provisions of the Act. The petition was dismissed and State of Maharashtra vide relevant notification directed attaching ofproperties of Respondent. In subsequent proceedings and furtherance thereto vide impugned judgment the subject notifications were set aside. Hence the present appeal.

**Held, while allowing the Appeal:**

The High Court has formed an erroneous opinion that firstly, only if the return includes interest, bonus or any other added benefit, it would be a deposit for the purpose of the MPID Act. However, Section 2(c) states that the return may be "with or without any benefit in the form of interest, bonus, profit or in any other form". The definition does not stipulate that there must be an added benefit, rather that the 'added benefit' is irrelevant for the purpose of the definition; secondly, that for the purpose of Section 2(c), the receipt of the commodity or money 'must be retained by itself'. The definition does not provide any such embargo. Rather, the definition is broadly worded to include even the possession of the commodities for a limited purpose. The High Court has read the definition of 'deposit' narrowly without any reference to the salutary purpose of the MPID Act.[61]

The High Court also made observations on the merits of the criminal proceedings. Referring to the role of NSEL in the default in payments, it observed that at the highest, the actions of NSEL would constitute offences under Sections 465 and 467 of the Indian Penal Code. The EOW filed a charge sheet under Section 173 Code of Criminal Procedure before the Sessions Judge, Special Court under the MPID Act for offences punishable under Sections 409, 465, 467, 468, 471, 474 and 477(4) read with Section 120(B). The High Court ought not to have made observations on the merits of the criminal proceedings when the writ petition was restricted to the issue of whether NSEL is a financial establishment for the purpose of the MPID Act.[62]

Further, while referring to the earlier order of the Division Bench dated 1 October 2015, where it was prima facie recorded that NSEL is a 'financial establishment' for the purpose of the MPID Act, the High Court observed that it was not bound by the prima facie view. The primary ground for the Division Bench for arriving at a prima facie view was the representations made assuring a 14% to 16% yield. However, the High Court in its impugned judgment dispelled the argument on the ground that only a 'faint reference' was made to assured returns. Such an observation misrepresents the factual instances which are backed by documentary material.[64]

Appeals thus allowed and the impugned judgment set aside. The impugned notifications issued under Section 4 of the MPID Act attaching the properties of the Respondent are valid.[66]

Disposition: Appeal Allowed

# Jaidev Rajnikant Shroff vs. Poonam Jaidev Shroff (03.12.2021 - SC) : MANU/SC/1179/2021

**Relative Section:**

Protection of Women from Domestic Violence Act, 2005 - Section 2(s)

**Hon'bleJudges/Coram:** L. Nageswara Rao and B.R. Gavai, JJ.

**Equivalent Citation:**

2021 (4) CCC 469 , 2021(4)Crimes434(SC), 2022 (2) MWN 467, 2022(1)RCR(Civil)290, (2022)1SCC683

**NumberofPagesintheOriginalJudgment: 9**

**Case Reference: nil**

**Case Note:**

Family - Divorce Proceedings -Domestic Violence - Living in shared household - Section 2(s) of the Protection of Women from Domestic Violence Act, 2005 (DV Act) - Cruelty - Wife (Respondent) left place of cohabitation with her Husband - Husband sought injunction against Wife entering into said house - Granted by Family Court - High Court vide impugned finding set aside said order in writ filed by Wife - Hence, the present appeal by Husband - Whether claim of Wife to enter into shared house or to be provided accommodation similar to husband's status sustainable?

**Facts:**

Appellant-husband sought divorce on the ground of cruelty. During the pendency of petition, husband lodged complaint against the Respondent-wife making certain serious allegations against her leading to registration of FIR. Thereafter, wife voluntarily left along with their daughter her mother's residence. Husband filed an application seeking restrain against wife from entering the house which was granted.High Court allowed the writ petition filed by wife challenging restrain order.

**Held, while dismissing the Applications:**

Relations between the parties are strained to such an extent that even the efforts made by Court to arrive at a settlement by personally discussing the matter in Chambers with them, have failed. On two occasions, this Court has appointed Mediators, who were Advocates. However, the mediation proceedings could not succeed. In such a situation, to compel the parties to live together in one house, would not be in the interest of either of the parties. [19]

To stretch the word 'similar' as used in the order, to be totally identical to the said house, would be unrealistic. It will be difficult to find out a house identical to the said house having the same area, the same facilities and the same luxuries. The word 'similar' has to be construed as providing the same degree of luxury and comfort as is available in the said house.[23]

The record and the pendency of the criminal proceedings would show that the relations between the parties are so strained that if they are permitted to live in the said house, it would lead to nothing else but further criminal proceedings.[24]

In the facts of present case, the injunction order need not be vacated.[26]

No merit in both the interlocutory applications and the same are rejected. In the event, the Respondent-wife decides to shift to any of the properties mentioned in the list annexed with the report of the Architect or she locates any of the rented premises as per her choice, the Appellant-husband shall pay the rent of the said premises from the date on which such premises are taken on rent.[28]

**Disposition:** Application Dismissed

# CHAPTER FOUR

# Kamatchi vs. Lakshmi Narayanan (13.04.2022-SC):MANU/SC/0471/2022

**Relative Sections:**

Child Marriage Restraint Act, 1929 - Section 9; Code of Civil Procedure, 1908 (CPC); Code of Criminal Procedure, 1973 (CrPC) - Section 2(d), Code of Criminal Procedure, 1973 (CrPC) - Section 4, Code of Criminal Procedure, 1973 (CrPC) - Section 5, Code of Criminal Procedure, 1973 (CrPC) - Section 190(1), Code of Criminal Procedure, 1973 (CrPC) - Section 200, Code of Criminal Procedure, 1973 (CrPC) - Section 202, Code of Criminal Procedure, 1973 (CrPC) - Section 203, Code of Criminal Procedure, 1973 (CrPC) - Section 468, Code of Criminal Procedure, 1973 (CrPC) - Section 468(2), Code of Criminal Procedure, 1973 (CrPC) - Section 469, Code of Criminal Procedure, 1973 (CrPC) - Section 470, Code of Criminal Procedure, 1973 (CrPC) - Section 473, Code of Criminal Procedure, 1973 (CrPC) - Section 482; Constitution of India - Article 14; Criminal Law (amendment) Act, 1952 - Section 6; Dowry Prohibition Act, 1961; Indian Penal Code, 1860 (IPC) - Section 498A; Prevention of Corruption Act, 1947; Protection Of Women From Domestic Violence Act, 2005 - Section 3, Protection Of Women From Domestic Violence Act, 2005 - Section 3(iv), Protection Of Women From Domestic Violence Act, 2005 - Section 12, Protection Of Women From Domestic Violence Act, 2005 - Section 12(1), Protection Of Women From Domestic Violence Act, 2005 - Section 17, Protection Of Women From Domestic Violence Act, 2005 - Section 18, Protection Of Women From Domestic Violence Act, 2005 - Section 19, Protection Of Women From Domestic Violence Act, 2005 - Section 20, Protection Of Women From Domestic Violence Act, 2005 - Section 21, Protection Of Women From Domestic Violence Act, 2005 - Section 22, Protection Of Women From Domestic Violence Act, 2005 - Section 23, Protection Of Women From Domestic Violence Act, 2005 -

Section 23(2), Protection Of Women From Domestic Violence Act, 2005 - Section 28, Protection Of Women From Domestic Violence Act, 2005 - Section 28(1), Protection Of Women From Domestic Violence Act, 2005 - Section 31, Protection Of Women From Domestic Violence Act, 2005 - Section 31(1), Protection Of Women From Domestic Violence Act, 2005 - Section 32; Protection Of Women From Domestic Violence Rules, 2006 - Rule 2(b), Protection Of Women From Domestic Violence Rules, 2006 - Rule 4(1), Protection Of Women From Domestic Violence Rules, 2006 - Rule 6(1), Protection Of Women From Domestic Violence Rules, 2006 - Rule 15(6)

**Hon'bleJudges/Coram:** U.U. Lalit and Pamidighantam Sri Narasimha, JJ.

**Equivalent Citation:**

2022(234)AIC79,AIR2022SC2932,2022(120)ACC282,2022 (2) ALT(Crl.) 254 (A.P.), 2022(2) Civil CC(S.C.) 2022(2)Crimes154(SC),2022(2)CriminalCC516,III(2022)DMC90SC, 2022GLH(2)703,2022(2)

HLR302,202/IN SC/ 422,2022(2)J.L.J.R.451,2022(3)JKJ74[SC],2022(3)KLT180,

2022(4)MLJ(Crl)228,2022(1)MWN (CR.) 593, 2022(2)PLJR413, 2022(2)RCR(Criminal)751,

2022(2)RLW1104(SC), 2022 (3) SCJ 286

**NumberofPagesintheOriginalJudgment: 20**

**Case Reference:**

Inderjit Singh Grewal v. State of Punjab and Ors. MANU/SC/0988/ 2011; Sarah Mathew and Ors. v. Institute of Cardio Vascular Diseases by its Director K.M. Cherian and Ors. MANU/SC/1210/2013; Adalat Prasad v. Rooplal Jindal and Ors. MANU/SC/0688/2004; A.R. Antulay v. Ramdas Sriniwas Nayak and Ors. MANU/SC/0082/1984; Bharat Damodar Kale and Ors. v. State of A.P. MANU/SC/0794/2003; Rashmi Kumar v. Mahesh Kumar Bhada MANU/SC/1052/1997; State of Himachal Pradesh v. Tara Dutt and Ors. MANU/SC/0729/1999; Japani Sahoo v. Chandra Sekhar Mohanty MANU/SC/3080/2007; U.P. Power Corporation Ltd. v. Ayodhya Prasad Mishra and Ors. MANU/SC/8042/2008; National Insurance Co. Ltd. v. Laxmi Narain Dhut MANU/SC/1233/2007; Murlidhar Meghraj Loya and Ors. v. State of Maharashtra and Ors. MANU/SC/0146/1976; Kisan Trimbak Kothula and Ors. v. State of Maharashtra MANU/SC/0133/1976; S. Amarjit Singh Kalra (dead) by Lrs. and Ors. v. Pramod Gupta (dead) by Lrs. and Ors. MANU/SC/1214/2002; N. Balaji v. Virendra Singh and

Ors. MANU/SC/0864/2004; Kailash v. Nanhku and Ors. MANU/SC/0264/2005; Meghmala and Ors. v. G. Narasimha Reddy and Ors. MANU/SC/0608/2010; State of Kerala v. M.K. Kunhikannan Nambiar Manjeri Manikoth, Naduvil (Dead) and Ors. MANU/SC/0240/1996; Tayabbhai M. Bagasarwalla and Ors. v. Hind Rubber Industries Pvt. Ltd. and Ors. MANU/SC/0280/1997; Noida Entrepreneurs Association and Ors. v. NOIDA and Ors. MANU/SC/0570/2011; Krishna Bhatacharjee v. Sarathi Choudhury and Ors. MANU/SC/1330/2015; Dr. P. Padmanathan and Ors. v. Tmt. V. Monica and Anr.; Krishna Pillai v. T.A. Rajendran and Anr. 1990 (Supp.) SCC 121; Alexander Rodger v. Comptoir D' Escompte (1871) LR 3 PC 465 : 17 ER 120; Sarah Mathew v. Institute of Cardio Vascular Diseases etc. and Ors. MANU/SC/0443/2014 : (2014) 2 SCC 102; Institute of Cardio Vascular Diseases v. Sarah Mathew, Criminal OP No. 12001 of 1997

**Case Note:**

Criminal - Quashing of proceedings - Section 12 of the Protection of Women from Domestic Violence Act, 2005 - Instant appeal is preferred by the Appellant against the order allowing the Petition filed by the Respondent and the proceedings against them were quashed - Whether High Court wrongly equated filing of an application under Section 12 of the Act to lodging of a complaint or initiation of prosecution?

**Facts:**

The present proceedings arise out of an application preferred by the Appellant under Section 12 of the Act, 2005. The application was filed seeking appropriate protection in terms of Sections 17 and 18 of the Act and was preferred against the Respondent-husband as well as the father-in-law and sister-in-law of the Appellant. The Petition filed by the father-in-law and the sister-in-law was allowed and the proceedings against them were quashed. The High Court took the view that the application ought to have been filed within one year of the incident and since the Appellant had left the matrimonial home in the year 2008, the application was abuse of process of the court. Appellant submits that, The limitation prescribed under Section 468 of the CrPC postulates that, no cognizance be taken by the Court more than a year after the commission of offence. Thus, the limitation is to be reckoned from the date of commission of offence.

**Held, while allowing the appeal**

1. It is, thus, clear that though Section 468 of the Code mandates that 'cognizance' ought to be taken within the specified period from the commission of offence, by invoking the principles of purposive

construction, this Court ruled that a complainant should not be put to prejudice, if for reasons beyond the control of the prosecuting agency or the complainant, the cognizance was taken after the period of limitation. It was observed by the Constitution Bench that if the filing of the complaint or initiation of proceedings was within the prescribed period from the date of commission of an offence, the Court would be entitled to take cognizance even after the prescribed period was over. [13]

2. The dictum in Sarah Mathew has to be understood in light of the situations which were dealt with by the Constitution Bench. If a complaint was filed within the period prescribed under Section 468 of the Code from the commission of the offence but the cognizance was taken after the expiry of such period, the terminal point for the prescribed period for the purposes of Section 468, was shifted from the date of taking cognizance to the filing of the complaint or initiation of proceedings so that a complaint ought not to be discarded for reasons beyond the control of the complainant or the prosecution. [14]

3. It is thus clear that the High Court wrongly equated filing of an application under Section 12 of the Act to lodging of a complaint or initiation of prosecution. The High Court was in error in observing that the application under Section 12 of the Act ought to have been filed within a period of one year of the alleged acts of domestic violence. [20]

4. It is, however, true that as noted by the Protection Officer in his Domestic Inspection Report dated 2.08.2018, there appears to be a period of almost 10 years after 16.09.2008, when nothing was alleged by the Appellant against the husband. But that is a matter which will certainly be considered by the Magistrate after response is received from the husband and the rival contentions are considered. That is an exercise which has to be undertaken by the Magistrate after considering all the factual aspects presented before him, including whether the allegations constitute a continuing wrong. The view taken by the High Court is quashed. Appeal allowed. [21]

**Disposition:** Appeal Allowed

# CHAPTER FIVE

# Satish Chander Ahuja vs. Sneha Ahuja(15.10.2020-SC) : MANU /SC/0767 /2020

**Relative Section:**

Code of Civil Procedure, 1908 (CPC) - Order I Rule 10, Code of Civil Procedure, 1908 (CPC) - Order XI Rule 12, Code of Civil Procedure, 1908 (CPC) - Order XI Rule 13, Code of Civil Procedure, 1908 (CPC) - Order XI Rule 14, Code of Civil Procedure, 1908 (CPC) - Order XII Rule 6; Code of Civil Procedure, 1908 (CPC) - Section 11, Code of Civil Procedure, 1908 (CPC) - Section 151; Code of Criminal Procedure, 1973 (CrPC) - Section 82, Code of Criminal Procedure, 1973 (CrPC) - Section 125, Code of Criminal Procedure, 1973 (CrPC) - Section 126, Code of Criminal Procedure, 1973 (CrPC) - Section 145, Code of Criminal Procedure, 1973 (CrPC) - Section 145(1), Code of Criminal Procedure, 1973 (CrPC) - Section 145(6), Code of Criminal Procedure, 1973 (CrPC) - Section 146, Code of Criminal Procedure, 1973 (CrPC) - Section 146(1), Code of Criminal Procedure, 1973 (CrPC) - Section 300, Code of Criminal Procedure, 1973 (CrPC) - Section 482; Constitution of India - Article 15(3), Constitution of India - Article 39, Constitution of India - Article 141, Constitution of India - Article 226, Constitution of India - Article 227; Consumer Protection Act, 1986 - Section 2(m); Family Law Act, 1996 - Section 30, Family Law Act, 1996 - Section 33, Family Law Act, 1996 - Section 40; Hindu Marriage Act, 1955 - Section 13(1); Hindu Adoption and Maintenance Act, 1956; Matrimonial Homes Act, 1967 - Section 1(1); Matrimonial Homes Act, 1983; Provincial Small Cause Courts Act, 1887; Indian Evidence Act, 1872 - Section 40, Indian Evidence Act, 1872 - Section 41, Indian Evidence Act,

1872 - Section 42, Indian Evidence Act, 1872 - Section 43, Indian Evidence Act, 1872 - Section 44; Indian Penal Code, 1860 (IPC) - Section 34, Indian Penal Code, 1860 (IPC) - Section 114, Indian Penal Code, 1860 (IPC) - Section 193, Indian Penal Code, 1860 (IPC) - Section 406, Indian Penal Code, 1860 (IPC) - Section 498A, Indian Penal Code, 1860 (IPC) - Section 506; Industrial Disputes Act, 1947 - Section 2(bb); Protection Of Women From Domestic Violence Act, 2005 - Section 2 (q), Protection Of Women From Domestic Violence Act, 2005 - Section 2(a), Protection Of Women From Domestic Violence Act, 2005 - Section 2(f), Protection Of Women From Domestic Violence Act, 2005 - Section 2(s), Protection Of Women From Domestic Violence Act, 2005 - Section 3, Protection Of Women From Domestic Violence Act, 2005 - Section 4, Protection Of Women From Domestic Violence Act, 2005 - Section 5, Protection Of Women From Domestic Violence Act, 2005 - Section 6, Protection Of Women From Domestic Violence Act, 2005 - Section 7, Protection Of Women From Domestic Violence Act, 2005 - Section 8, Protection Of Women From Domestic Violence Act, 2005 - Section 9, Protection Of Women From Domestic Violence Act, 2005 - Section 10, Protection Of Women From Domestic Violence Act, 2005 - Section 11, Protection Of Women From Domestic Violence Act, 2005 - Section 12, Protection Of Women From Domestic Violence Act, 2005 - Section 12(1), Protection Of Women From Domestic Violence Act, 2005 - Section 12(2), Protection Of Women From Domestic Violence Act, 2005 - Section 12(6), Protection Of Women From Domestic Violence Act, 2005 - Section 13, Protection Of Women From Domestic Violence Act, 2005 - Section 17, Protection Of Women From Domestic Violence Act, 2005 - Section 17(1), Protection Of Women From Domestic Violence Act, 2005 - Section 17(2), Protection Of Women From Domestic Violence Act, 2005 - Section 18, Protection Of Women From Domestic Violence Act, 2005 - Section 19, Protection Of Women From Domestic Violence Act, 2005 - Section 19(1), Protection Of Women From Domestic Violence Act, 2005 - Section 20, Protection Of Women From Domestic Violence Act, 2005 - Section 21, Protection Of Women From Domestic Violence Act, 2005 - Section 22, Protection Of Women From Domestic Violence Act, 2005 - Section 23, Protection Of Women From Domestic Violence Act, 2005 - Section 23(2), Protection Of Women From Domestic Violence Act, 2005 - Section 25, Protection Of Women From Domestic Violence Act, 2005 - Section 25(2), Protection Of Women From Domestic Violence Act, 2005 - Section 26, Protection Of Women From

Domestic Violence Act, 2005 - Section 26(1), Protection Of Women From Domestic Violence Act, 2005 - Section 26(3), Protection Of Women From Domestic Violence Act, 2005 - Section 28, Protection Of Women From Domestic Violence Act, 2005 - Section 28(1), Protection Of Women From Domestic Violence Act, 2005 - Section 28(2), Protection Of Women From Domestic Violence Act, 2005 - Section 29, Protection Of Women From Domestic Violence Act, 2005 - Section 31, Protection Of Women From Domestic Violence Act, 2005 - Section 36; Protection Of Women From Domestic Violence Rules, 2006 - Rule 5, Protection Of Women From Domestic Violence Rules, 2006 - Rule 6, Protection Of Women From Domestic Violence Rules, 2006 - Rule 6(4); Protection of Women from Domestic Violence Bill, 2005

**Hon'bleJudges/Coram:** Ashok Bhushan, R. Subhash Reddy and M.R. Shah, JJ.

**Equivalent Citation:** 2020(11)ADJ158, 2021(218)AIC161, AIR2020SC5397, 2020(6)ALD94, 2021 (145) ALR 218, 2020(6)ALT115, 2020 (3) ALT (Crl.) 368 (A.P.), 2020 6 AWC5516SC, 2020(6)BLJ436, 2020 (4) CCC 449 , 2020(4)Crimes238(SC), III(2020)DMC453SC, 2020GLH(4)416, 2020(3)HLR537, 2021(1)ICC1, ILR2020(4)Kerala421, 2020/INSC/599, 2020(4)J.L.J.R.188, 2020(5)JKJ1[SC], 2020(4)JLJ370, 2020 (5) KHC 496, 2020(6)KLT208, (2020)8MLJ48, 2020(4)PLJR211, 2020(4)RCR(Criminal)745, 2020(4)RLW3413(SC), (2021)1SCC414, [2020]12SCR189

**NumberofPagesintheOriginalJudgment: 54**

**Case Reference:**

S.R. Batra and Ors. v. Taruna Batra MANU/SC/0007/2007; Hiral P. Harsora and Ors. v. Kusum Narottamdas Harsora and Ors. MANU/SC/1269/2016; Vaishali Abhimanyu Joshi v. Nanasaheb Gopal Joshi MANU/SC/0626/2017; B.R. Mehta v. Atma Devi and Ors. MANU/SC/0740/1987; Kunapareddy v. Kunapareddy Swarna Kumari and Ors. MANU/SC/0628/2016; Ramesh Chander Kaushal v. Veena Kaushal and Ors. MANU/SC/0067/1978; Manmohan Attavar v. Neelam Manmohan Attavar MANU/SC/0808/2017; Bharat Co-Operative Bank (Mumbai) Ltd. v. Co-Operative Bank Employees Union MANU/SC/1574/2007; P. Kasilingam and Ors. v. P.S.G. College of Technology and Ors. MANU/SC/0265/1995; Pioneer Urban Land and Infrastructure Limited and Ors. v. Union of India (UOI) and Ors. MANU/SC/1071/2019; Jagir Singh and Ors. v. State of Bihar and Ors. MANU/SC/0387/1975; Mahalakshmi Oil Mills v. State of Andhra Pradesh

MANU/SC/0314/1988; Krishi Utpadan Mandi Samiti and Ors. v. Shankar Industries and Ors. MANU/SC/0729/1993; State of West Bengal v. Associated Contractors MANU/SC/0793/2014; The South Gujarat Roofing Tiles Manufacturers Association and Ors. v. The State of Gujarat and Ors. MANU/SC/0314/1976; Karnataka Power Transmission Corporation and Ors. v. Ashok Iron Works Pvt. Ltd. and Ors. MANU/SC/0158/2009; Reserve Bank of India v. Peerless General Finance and Investment Co. Ltd. and Ors. MANU/SC/0073/1987; Vimalben Ajitbhai Patel and Ors. v. Vatslabeen Ashokbhai Patel and Ors. MANU/SC/7334/2008; Deepika Kumar v. Medhavi Kumar and Ors. MANU/DE/3859/2015; Sangeeta v. Om Parkash Balyan and Ors. MANU/PH/1251/2015; Harish Chand Tandon v. Darpan Tandon and Ors. MANU/DE/3200/2015; Payal Sancheti and Ors. v. Harshvardhan Sancheti MANU/RH/0805/2008; N.S. Leelavathi and Ors. v. R. Shilpa Brunda MANU/KA/8874/2019; Maria Margarida Sequeria Fernandes and Ors. v. Erasmo Jack de Sequeria (Dead) through L. Rs. MANU/SC/0225/2012; Himani Alloys Ltd. v. Tata Steel Ltd. MANU/SC/0817/2011; S.M. Asif v. Virender Kumar Bajaj MANU/SC/0860/2015; Shanti Kumar Panda v. Shakuntala Devi MANU/SC/0863/2003; Razia Begum v. Sahebzadi Anwar Begum and Ors. MANU/SC/0003/1958; Ramesh Hirachand Kundanmal v. Municipal Corporation of Greater Bombay and Ors. MANU/SC/0493/1992; M.S. Sheriff v. The State of Madras and Ors. MANU/SC/0055/1954; S.M. Jakati and Ors. v. S.M. Borkar and Ors. MANU/SC/0148/1958; K.G. Premshanker v. Inspector of Police and Ors. MANU/SC/0771/2002; V.M. Shah v. State of Maharashtra and Ors. MANU/SC/0087/1996; Karam Chand Ganga Prasad and Ors. v. Union of India (UOI) and Ors. MANU/SC/0058/1970; Iqbal Singh Marwah and Ors. v. Meenakshi Marwah and Ors. MANU/SC/0197/2005; Ramdayal Jat v. Laxmi Prasad MANU/SC/0582/2009; Vishnu Dutt Sharma v. Daya Sapra MANU/SC/1101/2009; Kishan Singh (D) through Lrs. v. Gurpal Singh and Ors. MANU/SC/0591/2010; Eveneet Singh v. Prashant Chaudhri; Preeti Satija v. Raj Kumari and Anr.; Gough v. Gough (1891) 2 QB 665; Dilworth v. Stamps Commr. 1899 AC 99; S. Prabhakaran v. State of Kerala MANU/KE/0701/2008 : 2009 (2) RCR (Civil) 883; Navneet Arora v. Surender Kaur and Ors.; Sardar Malkiat Singh v. Knawaljit Kaur and Ors. MANU/DE/0714/2010 : 168 (2010) DLT 521; Neetu Mittal v. Kanta Mittal MANU/DE/1415/2008 : 2009 AIR (Del) 72; Sudha Mishra v. Surya Chand Mishra MANU/DE/2129/2014 : 2012 (3) AD (Delhi) 76; Ekta Arora v. Ajay Arora and Anr. MANU/DE/2234/2015 : AIR 2015 (Del) 180; Smt. Saloni Mahajn v.

Shri Madan Mohan Vig.; Smt. Chanchal Agarwal v. Jagdish Prasad Gupta and Anr.; A.R. Hashir Najyahouse and Ors. v. Shima and Ors.; Richa Gaur v. Kamal Kishore Gaur; Kolli Babi Sarojini and Ors. v. Kolli Jayalaxmi and Anr.; K. Subramani v. Director of Animal Husbandry, Chennai (2009) 1 MLJ 363

**Case Note:**

Family - 'Shared household' - Meaning thereof - Section 2(s) of the Protection of Women from Domestic Violence Act, 2005 (DV Act) - Right to Residence - Exercise thereof by Daughter-in-law in the property owned by Father-in-law - Determination thereof - Whether definition of shared household under Section 2(s) DV Act, 2005 to be read to mean that shared household can only be that household as household of joint family or wherein husband of the aggrieved person has a share? - Whether the law laid down by Supreme Court in the case of S.R. Batra and Anr. v. TarunaBatra does not lay down a correct law? - Appellant contended suit property exclusively owned by him is not a shared household and his son alongwith his wife were only gratuitous licencees - Respondent on the other hand contended that DV Act, 2005 granted protection and security of residence to woman - Respondent contended to be being in domestic relationship with the Appellant living in the suit property since her marriage and continues to do so till date, and property as shared household

Civil - Right to residence - Shared household - Property belonging to Father-in-law - Decree on Admission - Sustainability thereof - Order XII Rule 6 Code of Civil Procedure, 1908 (CPC) - Section 26 of Protection of Women from Domestic Violence Act, 2005 (DV Act) - Whether the High Court rightly concluded that suit filed by the Appellant could not have been decreed under Order XII Rule 6 Code of Civil Procedure? - Whether, when the Defendant (daughter-in-law) in her written statement pleaded that suit property is her shared household and she has right to residence therein, the Trial Court could have decreed the suit of the Plaintiff without deciding her such claim, permissible to be decided as per Section 26 of the Act, 2005?

Family - Definition of Respondent - 'Adult Male Person' - Domestic Relationship - Aggrieved Person - Section 2(q) of the Protection of Women from Domestic Violence Act, 2005 (DV Act) - Whether the Plaintiff in the suit giving rise to this appeal can be said to be the Respondent as per definition of Section 2(q) of DV Act?

Civil - Impleadment - Domestic Violence - Husband of Aggrieved Party - Order 1 Rule 10 of the Code of Civil Procedure, 1908 (CPC) Whether the husband of aggrieved party (Defendant) is necessary party in the suit filed by the Plaintiff (father-in-law) against the Defendant?

Civil - Jurisdiction - Enforceability and binding effect of Orders - Domestic Violence - Section 19 of the Protection of Women from Domestic Violence Act, 2005 (DV Act) - What is the effect of orders passed Under Section 19 of the Act, 2005 whether interim or final passed in the proceedings initiated in a civil court of competent jurisdiction?

**Facts:**

Appellant/ Plaintiff purchased property in question. His son got married to the Respondent and after marriage the Respondent started living in the first floor of the property in question along with her husband. Due to marital discord between them, Respondent moved out of the first floor and started staying in the guest room of the ground floor. She later started a separate kitchen in the first floor of the house. Her husband filed a Divorce Petition on the ground of cruelty against the Respondent and said proceeding is still pending. The Respondent after divorce petition was filed, moved an application under Section 12 of DV Act (as Complainant) impleading her husband as Respondent No. 1, Appellant as Respondent No. 2 and her mother in law as Respondent No. 3 alleging them to have caused severe emotional and mental abuses. In the application Respondent prayed for several orders and Trial Court while passing interim order held that Respondents shall not alienate the alleged shared household nor would they dispossess her or their children from the same without orders of a Competent Court. Appellant filed a Suit impleading her daughter-in-law as sole-Defendant for mandatory and permanent injunction and also for recovery of damages/mesne profit. Appellant pleaded that she had filed false and frivolous cases against him and his wife and hence sought removal of the Defendant from the suit property. Appellant also pleaded that his wife was subjected to various threats and violence in the hands of the Defendant on several occasions. Respondent/ Defendant (wife of Appellant's son) contested the suit stating that house property was acquired through joint family funds and thus not his self-acquired property. She further claimed suit property to be a shared household as per Section 2(s) of the DV Act and thus she has right to stay/reside in the shared household. Appellant sought decree on the basis of admission made by Respondent in application under Section 12 of DV Act as she has herself in her pleadings admitted him to be the owner of the suit property. Trial Court decreed the suit. High Court in appeal vide impugned order remanded the matter to the Trial Court for fresh adjudication in accordance with the directions given therein. Hence, the present appeal.

**Held, while dismissing the Appeals:**

The definition of shared household in Section 2(s) is an exhaustive definition. The first part of definition begins with expression "means" which is undoubtedly an exhaustive definition and second part of definition, which begins with word "includes" is explanatory of what was meant by the definition.[53]

The use of both the expressions "means and includes" in Section 2(s) of Act, 2005 clearly indicate the legislative intent that the definition is exhaustive and shall cover only those which fall within the purview of definition and no other. [54]

Right to residence under Section 19 is not an indefeasible right of residence in shared household especially when the daughter-in-law is pitted against aged father-in-law and mother-in-law. The senior citizens in the evening of their life are also entitled to live peacefully not haunted by marital discord between their son and daughter-in-law. While granting relief both in application under Section 12 of Act, 2005 or in any civil proceedings, the Court has to balance the rights of both the parties. The directions issued by High court adequately balances the rights of both the parties. [83]

The definition of shared household given in Section 2(s) cannot be read to mean that shared household can only be that household which is household of the joint family of which husband is a member or in which husband of the aggrieved person has a share. The judgment in S.R. Batra v. TarunaBatra has not correctly interpreted Section 2(s) of Act, 2005 and the judgment does not lay down a correct law. [84]

In view of the ratio laid down by this Court in the above case, the claim of the Defendant that suit property is shared household and she has right to reside in the house ought to have been considered by the Trial Court and non-consideration of the claim/defence is nothing but defeating the right, which is protected by Act, 2005. [96]

The power under Order XII Rule 6 is discretionary and cannot be claimed as a matter of right. In the facts of the present case, the Trial Court ought not to have given judgment under Order XII Rule 6 on the admission of the Defendant as contained in her application filed under Section 12 of the D.V. Act. Thus, there are more than one reason for not approving the course of action adopted by Trial Court in passing the judgment under Order XII Rule 6. Thus, High Court was correct that the judgment and decree of the Trial Court given under Order XII Rule 6 is unsustainable. [98]

For the purposes of determination of right of Defendant under Sections 17 and 19 read with Section 26 in the suit in question the Plaintiff can be treated as "Respondent", but for the grant of any relief to the Defendant or for successful resisting the suit of the Plaintiff necessary conditions for grant of relief as prescribed under the Act, 2005 has to be pleaded and proved by the Defendant, only then the relief can be granted by the Civil Court to the Defendant. [104]

The expression "save in accordance with the procedure established by law", in Section 17(2) of the Act, 2005 contemplates the proceedings in court of competent jurisdiction. Thus, suit for mandatory and permanent injunction/eviction or possession by the owner of the property is maintainable before a Competent Court. In Sub-section (2) the injunction is "shall not be evicted or excluded from the shared household save in accordance with procedure established by law". Thus, the provision itself contemplates adopting of any procedure established by law by the Respondent for eviction or exclusion of the aggrieved person from the shared household. Thus, in appropriate case, the competent court can decide the claim in a properly instituted suit by the owner as to whether the women need to be excluded or evicted from the shared household. The High Court in the impugned judgment has also expressed opinion that suit filed by the Plaintiff cannot be held to be non-maintainable which is correct. [116]

In case, the shared household of a woman is a tenanted/allotted/licensed accommodation where tenancy/allotment/license is in the name of husband, father-in-law or any other relative, the Act, 2005 does not operate against the landlord/lessor/licensor in initiating an appropriate proceedings for eviction of the tenant/allottee/licensee qua the shared household. However, in case the proceedings are due to any collusion between the two, the woman, who is living in the shared household has right to resist the proceedings on all grounds which the tenant/lessee/licensee could have taken in the proceedings. The embargo under Section 17(2) of Act, 2005 of not to be evicted or excluded save in accordance with the procedure established by law operates only against the "Respondent", i.e., one who is Respondent within the meaning of Section 2(q) of Act, 2005. [117]

Although husband of the Defendant was not a necessary party but in view of the pleadings in the written statement, the husband was a proper party. [122]

The order passed under D.V. Act whether interim or final shall be relevant and have to be given weight as one of evidence in the civil suit but the evidentiary value of such evidence is limited. The findings arrived therein by the magistrate although not binding on the Civil Court but the order having passed under the Act, 2005, which is an special Act has to be given its due weight.[154]

There is no embargo in referring to or relying on an admissible evidence, be of a civil court or criminal court both in civil or criminal proceedings. [156]

Accordingly, (i) the pendency of proceedings under Act, 2005 or any order interim or final passed under D.V. Act under Section 19 regarding right of residence not an embargo for initiating or continuing any civil proceedings, which relate to the subject matter of order interim or final passed in proceedings under D.V. Act, 2005. (ii) The judgment or order of criminal court granting an interim or final relief under Section 19 of D.V. Act, 2005 are relevant within the meaning of Section 43 of the Evidence Act and can be referred to and looked into by the civil court. (iii) A civil court is to determine the issues in civil proceedings on the basis of evidence, which has been led by the parties before the civil court. (iv) In the facts of the present case, suit filed in civil court for mandatory and permanent injunction was fully maintainable and the issues raised by the Appellant as well as by the Defendant claiming a right Under Section 19 were to be addressed and decided on the basis of evidence, which is led by the parties in the suit. [157]

High Court rightly set aside the decree of the Trial Court and remanded the matter for fresh adjudication. Appeal dismissed. [158]

**Disposition:** Appeal Dismissed

# CHAPTER SIX

# Rajnesh vs. Neha and Ors. (04.11.2020 – SC) : MANU/ SC/0833/2020

**Relative Section:**

Code of Civil Procedure, 1908 (CPC) - Order X, Code of Civil Procedure, 1908 (CPC) - Order XI, Code of Civil Procedure, 1908 (CPC) - Order XXI Rule 94; Code of Civil Procedure, 1908 (CPC) - Section 51, Code of Civil Procedure, 1908 (CPC) - Section 55, Code of Civil Procedure, 1908 (CPC) - Section 58, Code of Civil Procedure, 1908 (CPC) - Section 60, Code of Civil Procedure, 1908 (CPC) - Section 151; Code of Criminal Procedure, 1898 (CrPC) - Section 488, Code of Criminal Procedure, 1973 (CrPC) - Section 125, Code of Criminal Procedure, 1973 (CrPC) - Section 125(1), Code of Criminal Procedure, 1973 (CrPC) - Section 125(2), Code of Criminal Procedure, 1973 (CrPC) - Section 125(3), Code of Criminal Procedure, 1973 (CrPC) - Section 128, Code of Criminal Procedure, 1973 (CrPC) - Section 340, Code of Criminal Procedure, 1973 (CrPC) - Section 421; Constitution of India - Article 15(3), Constitution of India - Article 39, Constitution of India - Article 136, Constitution of India - Article 142; Family Courts Act, 1984 - Section 5, Family Courts Act, 1984 - Section 6, Family Courts Act, 1984 - Section 9, Family Courts Act, 1984 - Section 10, Family Courts Act, 1984 - Section 18; Hindu Adoptions And Maintenance Act, 1956 - Section 3(b), Hindu Adoptions And Maintenance Act, 1956 - Section 4(b), Hindu Adoptions And Maintenance Act, 1956 - Section 18, Hindu Adoptions And Maintenance Act, 1956 - Section 18(1), Hindu Adoptions And Maintenance Act, 1956 - Section 18(2), Hindu Adoptions And Maintenance Act, 1956 - Section 19, Hindu Adoptions And

Maintenance Act, 1956 - Section 20, Hindu Adoptions And Maintenance Act, 1956 - Section 20(3), Hindu Adoptions And Maintenance Act, 1956 - Section 22, Hindu Adoptions And Maintenance Act, 1956 - Section 23, Hindu Adoptions And Maintenance Act, 1956 - Section 23(2), Hindu Adoptions And Maintenance Act, 1956 - Section 23(3); Hindu Marriage Act, 1955 - Section 9, Hindu Marriage Act, 1955 - Section 10, Hindu Marriage Act, 1955 - Section 11, Hindu Marriage Act, 1955 - Section 12, Hindu Marriage Act, 1955 - Section 13, Hindu Marriage Act, 1955 - Section 14, Hindu Marriage Act, 1955 - Section 21, Hindu Marriage Act, 1955 - Section 24, Hindu Marriage Act, 1955 - Section 25, Hindu Marriage Act, 1955 - Section 25(1), Hindu Marriage Act, 1955 - Section 25(2), Hindu Marriage Act, 1955 - Section 26, Hindu Marriage Act, 1955 - Section 28A; Income-tax Act, 1961 - Section 10(26); Indian Evidence Act, 1872 - Section 106, Indian Evidence Act, 1872 - Section 165; Indian Penal Code, 1860 (IPC) - Section 191, Indian Penal Code, 1860 (IPC) - Section 193, Indian Penal Code, 1860 (IPC) - Section 199, Indian Penal Code, 1860 (IPC) - Section 209; Protection Of Women From Domestic Violence Act, 2005 - Section 2(a), Protection Of Women From Domestic Violence Act, 2005 - Section 2(f), Protection Of Women From Domestic Violence Act, 2005 - Section 2(q), Protection Of Women From Domestic Violence Act, 2005 - Section 2(s), Protection Of Women From Domestic Violence Act, 2005 - Section 3, Protection Of Women From Domestic Violence Act, 2005 - Section 12, Protection Of Women From Domestic Violence Act, 2005 - Section 12(1), Protection Of Women From Domestic Violence Act, 2005 - Section 17, Protection Of Women From Domestic Violence Act, 2005 - Section 17(1), Protection Of Women From Domestic Violence Act, 2005 - Section 17(2), Protection Of Women From Domestic Violence Act, 2005 - Section 18, Protection Of Women From Domestic Violence Act, 2005 - Section 19, Protection Of Women From Domestic Violence Act, 2005 - Section 19(1), Protection Of Women From Domestic Violence Act, 2005 - Section 20, Protection Of Women From Domestic Violence Act, 2005 - Section 20(1), Protection Of Women From Domestic Violence Act, 2005 - Section 20(2), Protection Of Women From Domestic Violence Act, 2005 - Section 20(6), Protection Of Women From Domestic Violence Act, 2005 - Section 21, Protection Of Women From Domestic Violence Act, 2005 - Section 22, Protection Of Women From Domestic Violence Act, 2005 - Section 23, Protection Of Women From Domestic Violence Act, 2005 - Section 26, Protection Of Women From Domestic Violence Act, 2005 - Section 26(1),

Protection Of Women From Domestic Violence Act, 2005 - Section 26(2), Protection Of Women From Domestic Violence Act, 2005 - Section 26(3), Protection Of Women From Domestic Violence Act, 2005 - Section 36; Special Marriage Act, 1954 - Section 4, Special Marriage Act, 1954 - Section 36, Special Marriage Act, 1954 - Section 37, Special Marriage Act, 1954 - Section 37(1); Marriage Laws (Amendment) Act, 2001; Indian Majority Act, 1875; Indian Divorce Act, 1869; Guardians and Wards Act, 1890; Hindu Minority and Guardianship Act, 1956; Hindu Marriage Act, 1956 - Section 28A

**Hon'bleJudges/Coram:** Indu Malhotra and R. Subhash Reddy, JJ.

**Equivalent Citation:** 2021(2)ACR1601, 2021(217)AIC70, AIR2021SC569, 2021(1)ALD216, 2021 (1) ALD(Crl.) 499 (SC), 2021 (114) ACC 645, 2021ALLMR(Cri)1172, 2020(6)ALT215, 2020 (3) ALT (Crl.) 464 (A.P.), 2021 4 AWC3465SC, 2021(1)BLJ1, 2020 (4) CCC 650 , 2020(4)Crimes291(SC), 2022(4) Crimes 371(SC), 2020(4)CriminalCC427, III(2020)DMC390SC, 2020GLH(4)727, 2020(3)HLR1, 2021(4)ICC757, ILR 2020(4)Kerala579, 2020/INSC/631, 2021(1)J.L.J.R.1, 2020(6)JKJ131[SC], 2020(4)JLJ481, 2020 (6) KHC 1, 2021(2)KLJ363, 2021-2-LW148, 2021- 1-LW(Crl)346, 2021(1)MLJ(Crl)124, 2021(3)MPLJ22, 2021 (1) MWN (CR.) 481, 2021(1)N.C.C.640, 2021(I)OLR348, 2021(1)PLJR1, (2020)200PLR793, 2020(4)RCR(Criminal)879, 2021(3)RLW1871(SC), (2021)2SCC324, 2021 (1) SCJ 444, [2020]13SCR1093

**NumberofPagesintheOriginalJudgment: 48**

**Case Reference:**

Ramesh Chander Kaushal v. Veena Kaushal and Ors. MANU/SC/0067/ 1978; Nanak Chand v. Chandra Kishore Aggarwal and Ors. MANU/SC/ 0481/1969; Ram Singh v. State and Anr. MANU/UP/0099/1963; Nalini Ranjan Chakravarty v. Kiran Rani Chakravarty MANU/BH/0128/1965; Chand Dhawan v. Jawaharlal Dhawan MANU/SC/0538/1993; Bhagwan Dutt v. Kamla Devi and Ors. MANU/SC/0205/1974; Chaturbhuj v. Sita Bai MANU/SC/8141/2007; Bhuwan Mohan Singh v. Meena MANU/SC/ 0605/2014; Hiral P. Harsora and Ors. v. Kusum Narottamdas Harsora and Ors. MANU/SC/1269/2016; D. Velusamy v. D. Patchaiammal MANU/SC/ 0872/2010; Indra Sarma v. V.K.V. Sarma MANU/SC/1230/2013; S.R. Batra and Ors. v. Taruna Batra MANU/SC/0007/2007; Ashok Singh Pal v. Smt. Manjulata MANU/MP/0007/2008; Mohan Swaroop Chauhan v. Mohini MANU/MP/1262/2015; RD v. BD MANU/DE/2483/2019; Nagendrappa

Natikar v. Neelamma MANU/SC/0248/2013; Sudeep Chaudhary v. Radha Chaudhary MANU/SC/1699/1997; Puneet Kaur v. Inderjit Singh Sawhney MANU/DE/7166/2011; Kusum Sharma v. Mahinder Kumar Sharma MANU/DE/2406/2017; Manish Jain v. Akanksha Jain MANU/SC/0355/2017; Sh. Bharat Hegde v. Smt. Saroj Hegde MANU/DE/1518/2007; Sunita Kachwaha v. Anil Kachwaha MANU/SC/0964/2014; Chander Parkash Bodh Raj v. Shila Rani Chander Prakash MANU/DE/0028/1968; Shamima Farooqui v. Shahid Khan MANU/SC/0380/2015; Kanhu Charan Jena v. Nirmala Jena MANU/OR/0326/2000; Krishna w/o Dharam Raj Jain v. Dharam Raj s/o Laxmi Chand Jain MANU/MP/0156/1991; Ganga Prasad Srivastava v. Additional District Judge, Gonda and Ors. MANU/UP/1905/2019; S. Radhakumari v. K.M.K. Nair MANU/KE/0031/1983; Samir Kr. Banerjee v. Sujata Banerjee MANU/WB/0386/1965; Kalpana Das and Ors. v. Sarat Kumar Das MANU/OR/0180/2009; Shail Kumari Devi and Ors. v. Krishan Bhagwan Pathak MANU/SC/3353/2008; Badshah v. Urmila Badshah Godse and Ors. MANU/SC/1084/2013; Smt. Sushila Viresh Chhadva v. Viresh Nagshi Chhadva MANU/MH/0021/1996; Bani v. Parkash Singh MANU/PH/0028/1996; Mohinder Verma v. Sapna MANU/PH/3684/2014; Shri Satish Kumar v. Meena MANU/DE/0771/2001; Smt. Santosh Sehgal v. Shri Murari Lal Sehgal MANU/DE/2213/2006; Chanmuniya v. Chanmuniya Virendra Kumar Singh Kushwaha and Ors. MANU/SC/0807/2010; Kamala and Ors. v. M.R. Mohan Kumar MANU/SC/1203/2018; Jasbir Kaur Sehgal v. District Judge, Dehradun and Ors. MANU/SC/0835/1997; Vinny Parmvir Parmar v. Parmvir Parmar MANU/SC/0842/2011; Reema Salkan v. Sumer Singh Salkan MANU/SC/1043/2018; Shailja and Ors. v. Khobbanna MANU/SC/0537/2017; P. Suresh v. S. Deepa and Ors. MANU/KA/0721/2016; K. Sivaram v. K. Mangalamba and Ors. MANU/AP/0017/1989; Gurvinder Singh v. Murti and Ors. MANU/PH/0138/1990; Venkateshwar Dwivedi v. Ruchi Dwivedi and Ors. MANU/MP/1083/2017; Davis v. Thomas MANU/KE/0675/2007; Sakeer Hussain T.P. v. Naseera and Ors. MANU/KE/1627/2016; Mahabir Agarwalla v. Gita Roy MANU/WB/0244/1961 : (1962) 2 Cr. L.J. 528; Abhilasha v. Parkash and Ors. Criminal Appeal No. 615/2020; Satish Chander Ahuja v. Sneha Ahuja Civil Appeal No. 2483/2020; Sujit Adhikari v. Tulika Adhikari; Chandra Mohan Das v. Tapati Das; Vishal v. Aparna and Anr.; Tanushree and Ors. v. A.S. Moorthy; Rakesh Malhotra v. Krishna Malhotra; Kusum Sharma v. Mahinder Kumar Sharma MANU/DE/2910/2014 : (2014) 214 DLT 493; Kusum Sharma II Case MANU/DE/0155/2015 : (2015) 217 DLT

706; Susmita Mohanty v. Rabindra Nath Sahu MANU/OR/0176/1996 : 1996 (I) OLR 361; Arun Kumar Nayak v. Urmila Jena MANU/OR/0082/ 2010 : (2010) 93 AIC 726 (Ori); Bina Devi v. State of U.P. MANU/UP/0057/ 2010 : (2010) 69 ACC 19; Gouri Das v. Pradyumna Kumar Das MANU/OR/ 0189/1986 : 1986 (II) OLR 44; Kaushalya v. Mukesh Jain Criminal Appeal Nos. 1129-1130/2019; Amit Verma v. Sangeeta Verma and Ors. CRR No. 3542/2019; Satish Kumar v. Meena; Panditrao Chimaji Kalure v. Gayabai MANU/MH/0039/2002 : (2002) 2 Mah LJ 53; Bina Devi and Ors. v. State of Uttar Pradesh and Ors. MANU/UP/0057/2010 : (2010) 69 ACC 19; Sanjay Damodar Kale v. Kalyani Sanjay Kale; Lavlesh Shukla v. Rukmani Crl. Rev. P. 851/2019; Vipul Lakhanpal v. Smt. Pooja Sharma; Kusum Sharma IV Case MANU/DE/6474/2017 : 2017 - (2018) 246 DLT 1

**Case Note:**

Family - Maintenance - Guidelines thereto - Respondent No. 1-wife left matrimonial home shortly after birth of son-Respondent No. 2 - Wife filed application for interim maintenance under Section 125 of Code on behalf of herself and minor son - Family Court awarded interim maintenance to Respondent No. 1-wife and Respondent No. 2-son - Appellant-husband challenged Order of Family Court filed before High Court - High Court dismissed Writ Petition and affirmed Judgment passed by Family Court - Hence, present appeal - Whether there was need to frame guidelines on certain aspects pertaining to payment of maintenance in matrimonial matters.

**Facts:**

The Respondent No. 1-wife left matrimonial home shortly after the birth of the son-Respondent No. 2. The wife filed an application for interim maintenance under Section 125 Code of Criminal Procedure on behalf of herself and the minor son. The Family Court vide a detailed Order awarded interim maintenance to the Respondent No. 1-wife and Respondent No. 2-son. The Appellant-husband challenged the Order of the Family Court vide Criminal Writ Petition filed before the High Court, Nagpur Bench. The High Court dismissed the Writ Petition and affirmed the Judgment passed by the Family Court. This Court issued notice to the wife and directed the Appellant-husband to file his Income Tax Returns and Assessment Orders. He was also directed to place a photocopy of his passport on record. By a further Order, the Appellant-husband was directed to make payment of the arrears towards interim maintenance to the wife and a further amount which was due and payable to the wife towards arrears of maintenance, as per his own admission. By a subsequent Order, it was recorded that only a part of the arrears had been paid. A final opportunity was granted to the Appellant-husband to make payment of the balance amount, failing which, the Court would proceed under the Contempt of Courts Act for wilful disobedience with the Orders passed by this Court. In the backdrop of the facts of this case, it was fit to frame guidelines on certain aspects pertaining to the payment of maintenance in matrimonial matters.

**Held, while disposing off the appeal:**

(i) The Judgment and order passed by the Family Court, affirmed by the High Court for payment of interim maintenance to the Respondent No. 1-wife, and Respondent No. 2-son, was affirmed by this Court. The husband was directed to pay the entire arrears of maintenance within a period of twelve weeks from the date of this Judgment, and continue to comply with this Order during the pendency of the proceedings under Section 125 Code of Criminal Procedure before the Family Court. If the Appellant-husband fails to comply with the said directions of this Court, it would be open to the Respondents to have the Order enforced under Section 128 Code of Criminal Procedure, and take recourse to all other remedies which are available in accordance with law. [1]

(ii) To overcome the issue of overlapping jurisdiction, and avoid conflicting orders being passed in different proceedings, it had become necessary to issue directions in this regard, so that there was uniformity in the practice followed by the Family Courts/District Courts/Magistrate Courts throughout the country. It was directed that

(a) where successive claims for maintenance were made by a party under different statutes, the Court would consider an adjustment or set-off, of the amount awarded in the previous proceeding/s, while determining whether any further amount was to be awarded in the subsequent proceeding.

(b) it was made mandatory for the Applicant to disclose the previous proceeding and the orders passed therein, in the subsequent proceeding.

(c) if the order passed in the previous proceeding/s requires any modification or variation, it would be required to be done in the same proceeding. [98]

(iii) The Affidavit of Disclosure of Assets and Liabilities annexed of this judgment, as may be applicable, shall be filed by both parties in all maintenance proceedings, including pending proceedings before the concerned Family Court/District Court/Magistrates Court, as the case may be, throughout the country. [99]

(iv) For determining the quantum of maintenance payable to an applicant, the Court shall take into account the criteria enumerated in Part B - III of the judgment. [100]

(v) The maintenance in all cases will be awarded from the date of filing the application for maintenance. [102]

(vi) For enforcement/execution of orders of maintenance, it was directed that an order or decree of maintenance may be enforced under Section 28A of the Hindu Marriage Act, 1956 (sic1955), Section 20(6) of the D.V. Act and Section 128 of Code of Criminal Procedure, as may be applicable. The order of maintenance may be enforced as a money decree of a civil court as per the provisions of the Code of Civil Procedure, more particularly Sections 51, 55, 58, 60 read with Order 21. [103]

# CHAPTER SEVEN

# S. Vanitha vs. The Deputy Commissioner, Bengaluru Urban District and Ors. (15.12.2020 - SC) : MANU/SC/0943/2020

**Relative Section:**

Code of Criminal Procedure, 1973 (CrPC) - Section 195; Constitution of India - Article 14, Constitution of India - Article 15, Constitution of India - Article 21, Constitution of India - Article 136, Constitution of India - Article 142, Constitution of India - Article 226; Hindu Marriage Act, 1955 - Section 13(1), Hindu Marriage Act, 1955 - Section 28; Indian Penal Code, 1860 (IPC) - Section 498A; Maintenance And Welfare Of Parents And Senior Citizens Act 2007 - Section 2, Maintenance And Welfare Of Parents And Senior Citizens Act 2007 - Section 2(b), Maintenance And Welfare Of Parents And Senior Citizens Act 2007 - Section 2(f), Maintenance And Welfare Of Parents And Senior Citizens Act 2007 - Section 2(g), Maintenance And Welfare Of Parents And Senior Citizens Act 2007 - Section 3, Maintenance And Welfare Of Parents And Senior Citizens Act 2007 - Section 4, Maintenance And Welfare Of Parents And Senior Citizens Act 2007 - Section 4(i), Maintenance And Welfare Of Parents And Senior Citizens Act 2007 - Section 5, Maintenance And Welfare Of Parents And Senior Citizens Act 2007 - Section 5(1), Maintenance And Welfare Of Parents And Senior Citizens Act 2007 - Section 6, Maintenance And Welfare Of Parents And Senior Citizens Act 2007 - Section 6, Maintenance And Welfare

Of Parents And Senior Citizens Act 2007 - Section 7, Maintenance And Welfare Of Parents And Senior Citizens Act 2007 - Section 8, Maintenance And Welfare Of Parents And Senior Citizens Act 2007 - Section 8(1), Maintenance And Welfare Of Parents And Senior Citizens Act 2007 - Section 8(2), Maintenance And Welfare Of Parents And Senior Citizens Act 2007 - Section 9, Maintenance And Welfare Of Parents And Senior Citizens Act 2007 - Section 9(1), Maintenance And Welfare Of Parents And Senior Citizens Act 2007 - Section 10, Maintenance And Welfare Of Parents And Senior Citizens Act 2007 - Section 11, Maintenance And Welfare Of Parents And Senior Citizens Act 2007 - Section 23, Maintenance And Welfare Of Parents And Senior Citizens Act 2007 - Section 23(1), Maintenance And Welfare Of Parents And Senior Citizens Act 2007 - Section 23(2), Maintenance And Welfare Of Parents And Senior Citizens Act 2007 - Section 27; Protection Of Women From Domestic Violence Act, 2005 - Section 2, Protection Of Women From Domestic Violence Act, 2005 - Section 2(q), Protection Of Women From Domestic Violence Act, 2005 - Section 2(s), Protection Of Women From Domestic Violence Act, 2005 - Section 12(1), Protection Of Women From Domestic Violence Act, 2005 - Section 17, Protection Of Women From Domestic Violence Act, 2005 - Section 18, Protection Of Women From Domestic Violence Act, 2005 - Section 19, Protection Of Women From Domestic Violence Act, 2005 - Section 20, Protection Of Women From Domestic Violence Act, 2005 - Section 21, Protection Of Women From Domestic Violence Act, 2005 - Section 22, Protection Of Women From Domestic Violence Act, 2005 - Section 26, Protection Of Women From Domestic Violence Act, 2005 - Section 26(1), Protection Of Women From Domestic Violence Act, 2005 - Section 26(3), Protection Of Women From Domestic Violence Act, 2005 - Section 36; Recovery Of Debts And Bankruptcy, Insolvency Resolution And Bankruptcy Of Individuals And Partnership Firms Act, 1993 - Section 34; Special Court (trial Of Offences Relating To Transactions In Securities) Act, 1992 - Section 9A, Special Court (trial Of Offences Relating To Transactions In Securities) Act, 1992 - Section 13

**Hon'bleJudges/Coram:** Dr. D.Y. Chandrachud, Indu Malhotra and Indira Banerjee, JJ.

**EquivalentCitation :**

2021(1)ADJ347,2021(217)AIC20,

AIR2021SC177,2021(2)ALD17,2021(144)ALR 762 , 2021(1)BLJ204, 2021 (1) CCC 1 , 2021(1)Crimes53(SC), I(2021)DMC3SC,

(2021)1GLR784, 2021 (1) HLR98, 2021(1)ICC53, 2020/INSC/701, 2021(1)J.L.J.R.353, 2021(1)JLJ376, 2021(3)KarLJ347, 2020 (6) KHC 749, 2021(1)KLJ609, 2021(1)KLT80, 2021(5)MhLj39, (2021)1MLJ431, 2021(2)MPLJ584, 2021(1)PLJR373, (2021)201PLR117, 2021 151 RD116, (2021)15SCC730, [2020]12SCR1057

**NumberofPagesintheOriginalJudgment: 20**

**Case Reference:**

Jagir Singh and Ors. v. State of Bihar and Ors. MANU/SC/0387/1975; Bharat Co-Operative Bank (Mumbai) Ltd. v. Co-Operative Bank Employees Union MANU/SC/1574/2007; Paul Enterprises and Ors. v. Rajib Chatterjee and Co. and Ors. MANU/SC/0031/2009; Bank of India v. Ketan Parekh and Ors. MANU/SC/2700/2008; Pioneer Urban Land and Infrastructure Limited and Ors. v. Union of India (UOI) and Ors. MANU/SC/1071/2019; Solidaire India Ltd. v. Fairgrowth Financial Services Ltd. and Ors. MANU/SC/0009/2001; Satish Chander Ahuja v. Sneha Ahuja Civil Appeal No. 2483 of 2020; Kasilingam v. P.S.G. College of Technology

**Case Note:**

Family - Eviction - Shared household - Section 23 (2) of Senior Citizen Act 2007 and Section 2 of Protection of Women from Domestic Violence Act 2005 - Second and Third Respondents filed application under provisions of Maintenance and Welfare of Parents and Senior Citizens Act 2007 and inter alia, sought Appellant and her daughter's eviction from residential house - Assistant Commissioner, and Deputy Commissioner in appeal, allowed application and directed Appellant to vacate suit premises - Aggrieved by this order, Appellant pursued writ proceeding before Single Judge, and in appeal before Division Bench of High Court - Division Bench held that suit premises belonged to mother-in-law (Second Respondent) of Appellant - Division Bench upheld Order of Deputy Commissioner, and directed Appellant to vacate suit premises - Hence, present appeal - Whether impugned order of ousting Appellant as daughter-in-law and minor daughter was suffer from any infirmity.

**Facts:**

The Second and Third Respondents filed an application under the provisions of the Maintenance and Welfare of Parents and Senior Citizens Act 2007, and inter alia, sought the Appellant and her daughter's eviction from a residential house. The Assistant Commissioner, and the Deputy Commissioner in appeal, allowed the application under the Senior Citizens Act 2007 and directed the Appellant to vacate the suit premises. Aggrieved by this order, the Appellant unsuccessfully pursued a writ proceeding before a Single Judge, and in appeal before a Division Bench of the High Court of Karnataka. The Division Bench held that the suit premises belonged to the mother-in-law (the Second Respondent) of the Appellant and the remedy of the Appellant for maintenance and shelter lies only against her estranged husband (the Fourth Respondent). The Division Bench upheld the Order of the Deputy Commissioner, and directed the Appellant to vacate the suit premises.

**Held, while allowing the appeal:**

(i) Both pieces of legislation are intended to deal with salutary aspects of public welfare and interest. The PWDV Act 2005 was intended to deal with the problems of domestic violence which, as the Statements of Objects and Reasons sets out, is widely prevalent but has remained largely invisible in the public domain. The Statements of Objects and Reasons indicates that while Section 498A of the Indian Penal Code created a penal offence out of a woman's subjection to cruelty by her husband or relative, the civil law did not address its phenomenon in its entirety. Hence, consistent with the provisions of Articles 14, 15 and 21 of the Constitution, Parliament enacted a legislation which would provide for a remedy under the civil law which is intended to protect the woman from being victims of domestic violence and to prevent the occurrence of domestic violence in the society. The ambit of the Bill indicates that a significant object of the legislation is to provide for and recognize the rights of women to secure housing and to recognize the right of a woman to reside in a matrimonial home or a shared household, whether or not she has any title or right in the shared household. Allowing the Senior Citizens Act 2007 to have an overriding force and effect in all situations, irrespective of competing entitlements of a woman to a right in a shared household within the meaning of the PWDV Act 2005, would defeat the object and purpose which the Parliament sought to achieve in enacting the latter legislation. The law protecting the interest of senior citizens is intended to ensure that they are not left destitute, or at the mercy of their children or relatives. Equally, the purpose of the PWDV Act 2005 cannot be ignored by a sleight of statutory interpretation. Both sets of legislations have to be harmoniously construed. Hence the right of a woman to secure a residence order in respect of a shared household cannot be defeated by the simple expedient of securing an order of eviction by adopting the summary procedure under the Senior Citizens Act 2007. [21]

(ii) On construing the provisions of Sub-section (2) of Section 23 of the Senior Citizen Act 2007, it was evident that it applies to a situation where a senior citizen had a right to receive maintenance out of an estate and such estate or part thereof is transferred. On the other hand, the Appellant's simple plea was that the suit premises constitute her shared household within the meaning of Section 2 of the PWDV Act 2005. The series of transactions which took place in respect of the property, the spouse of the Appellant purchased it in his own name a few months before the marriage but subsequently sold it, after a few years, under a registered sale deed at the same price to his father (the father-in-law of the Appellant), who in turn gifted it to his spouse i.e. the mother-in-law of the Appellant after divorce proceedings were instituted by the Fourth Respondent. Parallel to this, the Appellant had instituted proceedings of dowry harassment against her mother-in-law and her estranged spouse and her spouse had instituted divorce proceedings. The Appellant had also filed proceedings for maintenance against the Fourth Respondent and the divorce proceedings are pending. It is subsequent to these events, that the Second and Third Respondents instituted an application under the Senior Citizens Act 2007. The fact that specific proceedings under the PWDV Act 2005 had not been instituted when the application under the Senior Citizens Act, 2007 was filed, should not lead to a situation where the enforcement of an order of eviction deprives her from pursuing her claim of entitlement under the law. The inability of a woman to access judicial remedies may, as this case exemplifies, be a consequence of destitution, ignorance or lack of resources. Even otherwise, recourse to the summary procedure contemplated by the Senior Citizen Act 2007 was not available for the purpose of facilitating strategies that are designed to defeat the claim of the Appellant in respect of a shared household. A shared household would have to be interpreted to include the residence where the Appellant had been jointly residing with her husband. Merely because the ownership of the property has been subsequently transferred to her in-laws (Second and Third Respondents) or that her estranged spouse (Fourth Respondent) was now residing separately, was no ground to deprive the Appellant of the protection that was envisaged under the PWDV Act 2005. [23]

(iii) The claim of the Appellant that the premises constitute a shared household within the meaning of the PWDV Act 2005 would have to be determined by the appropriate forum. The claim could not simply be obviated by evicting the Appellant in exercise of the summary powers entrusted by the Senior Citizens Act 2007. The Second and Third Respondents were at liberty to make a subsequent application under Section 10 of the Senior Citizens Act 2007 for alteration of the maintenance allowance, before the appropriate forum. [24]

**Ratio Decidendi:**

The right of a woman to secure a residence order in respect of a shared household cannot be defeated by the simple expedient of securing an order of eviction by adopting the summary procedure under the Senior Citizens Act 2007.

**Disposition:** Appeal Allowed

# Aishwarya Atul Pusalkar vs. Maharashtra Housing and Area Development Authority and Ors. (27.04.2020 - SC) : MANU/SC/0414/2020

**Relative Section:**

Constitution of India - Article 142, Constitution of India - Article 226; Hindu Adoptions And Maintenance Act, 1956 - Section 18; Maharashtra Housing And Area Development Act, 1976 - Section 2(25), Maharashtra Housing And Area Development Act, 1976 - Section 79, Maharashtra Housing And Area Development Act, 1976 - Section 95A, Maharashtra Housing And Area Development Act, 1976 - Section 95A(1), Maharashtra Housing And Area Development Act, 1976 - Section 177; Protection Of Women From Domestic Violence Act, 2005 - Section 2(s), Protection Of Women From Domestic Violence Act, 2005 - Section 3(iv), Protection Of Women From Domestic Violence Act, 2005 - Section 19

**Hon'bleJudges/Coram:** Deepak Gupta and Aniruddha Bose, JJ.

**Equivalent Citation:** 2020(5)ABR480, AIR2020SC4238, 2020(5)ALD33, 2020(4)ALLMR644, 2020(4) BL J76, 2021(1)BomCR771, 2020 (2) CCC 461 , 2020(3)CTC757, 2020(II)CLR(SC)669, 2020(3)HLR245, 2020/ INSC/369, (2020)17SCC313, [2020]6SCR342

**NumberofPagesintheOriginalJudgment: 19**

**Case Reference:** Aishwarya Atul Pusalkar v. Atul Shivram Pusalkar and Anr. Civil App. No. 183 of 2004

**Case Note:**

Family - Matrimonial home - Right to reside - Family of Appellant's husband (Respondent No. 8) were owners of said plot, on which stood the residential building - Said building upon demolition was redeveloped by firm of builders and during period of redevelopment, occupants were required to shift to transit or temporary accommodations - Certain arrangement was entered into between builder and family of Appellant's husband - There was dispute as regards actual area of allocation to Respondent No. 8 and his family by Respondent No. 7 in new building - There had been certain parallel developments pertaining to Appellant's matrimonial dispute with her husband - In said dispute, High Court set aside decree of judicial separation passed by Family Court in favour of Respondent No.8/husband - Complaint of Appellant was that after decree of judicial separation was invalidated, her husband and his family had not allowed her to reside in flats allocated to them in redeveloped building - Appellant thereafter filed writ petition in High Court - High Court held that right which Appellant was seeking to establish could not be enforced invoking writ jurisdiction of Court - Hence, present appeal - Whether Appellant entitled for any relief in respect of right to reside in matrimonial home.

**Facts:**

The family of Appellant's husband (Respondent No. 8) were originally the owners of the said plot, on which a residential building was stood. Said building upon demolition was redeveloped by a firm of builders. During the period of redevelopment, the occupants were required to shift to transit or temporary accommodations. There was certain arrangement entered into between the builder and the family of the Appellant's husband. There was dispute as regards actual area of allocation to the Respondent No. 8 and his family by the Respondent No. 7 in the new building. There had been certain parallel developments pertaining to the Appellant's matrimonial dispute with her husband. In the Family Court, the Husband/Respondent No. 8 had been granted a decree of judicial separation. His plea for divorce was not accepted by the Family Court. The decree of judicial separation was passed. Both the Appellant and the Respondent No. 8 appealed against the said judgment and decree before the High Court. The High Court had allowed the Appellant's appeal and set aside the decree of judicial separation. The appeal of her husband against the Family Court's judgment refusing to grant divorce was dismissed. This decision was delivered by the High Court after she had shifted to her temporary accommodation. The complaint of the Appellant was that after the decree of judicial separation was invalidated, her husband and his family had not allowed her to reside in the flats allocated to them in the redeveloped building. She claims in substance that such refusal was in breach of her right to reside in her matrimonial home. It was also her case that as she had vacated the original residential unit on the basis of a statutory notice, she had her right to be rehoused in those flats as part of statutory rehabilitation measure. The Appellant thereafter filed the writ petition in the High Court. The High Court in the judgment under appeal sustained the plea of the Respondents that the right which the Appellant was seeking to establish could not be enforced invoking writ jurisdiction of the Court.

**Held, while disposing off the appeal:**

(i) This Court recognises the Appellant's right to reside in her matrimonial home. Such right had a legitimate basis. Though the enforcement mechanism adopted by her to enforce her right was not legally acceptable, a brief discussion on the right she was seeking to enforce was necessary to understand the scope of her claim. A married woman was entitled to live, subsequent to her marriage, with rest of her family members on the husband's side, in case it was a joint-property. If she resides in an accommodation as an independent family unit with her husband and children, the matrimonial home would be that residential unit. This right is embedded in her right as a wife. It is implicit under the provisions of Section 18 of the Hindu Adoption and Maintenance Act, 1956 in situations that statute was applicable. The Protection of Women from Domestic Violence Act, 2005 had recognized the concept of shared household in terms of Section 2(s) of this statute. Alienating an immovable asset to defeat the right of a victim lady under the said Act can constitute domestic violence, coming, inter-alia, within the ambit of the expression economic abuse under Section 3(iv) of 2005 Act. A Magistrate having jurisdiction under Section 19 of the said Act is empowered to pass a residence order to protect a victim of domestic violence from being removed from her shared household. But for a husband to compel his wife to live in a separate household, which was not her matrimonial home, an order from appropriate legal forum would be necessary. There could not be forcible dishousing of a wife from her matrimonial home. [9]

(ii) There appears to be some matters pending in different fora in relation to the matrimonial dispute between the Appellant and the Respondent No. 8. The position as it stands now was that the decree of judicial separation stands invalidated and as of now, the Appellant was the legally wedded wife of the Respondent No. 8. She had been out of her matrimonial home. But such right could not be enforced invoking the writ jurisdiction. Moreover, the original building that constituted her matrimonial home had been demolished. Large portions of the redeveloped building on the same plot had been parted with. Now going by its traditional meaning, her matrimonial home at present would be the premises in which her husband was residing. In this complex perspective, a judicial forum having fact-finding jurisdiction would be the proper forum for adjudicating her claim of this nature. The Appellant drew attention to Section 177 of the Maharashtra Housing and Area Development Act, 1976 to contend that disputes arising out of the said Act could not be adjudicated upon by a Civil Court. The dispute raised by her did not arise out of any of the provisions of the 1976 Act. Though she was dishoused as an occupier applying the provisions of the 1976 Act, claim of her rehousing was based on her status as wife of the Respondent No. 8. Such claim had to be adjudicated upon by the Civil Court or the Family Court or any other forum the law may prescribe. Such right of the Appellant could not be diffused with the right of her husband under the 1976 Act, whose family property, part of which he was the owner, had been reconstructed. [11]

(iii) Considering the fact that the dispute was pending for a very long time, this court shall be giving certain directions in exercise of our jurisdiction under Article 142 of the Constitution of India which would conclude the dispute. This court shall do so having regard to the fact that the builder and the husband of the Appellant have uniformly stated that flat was available to accommodate the Appellant. For this reason, the Appellant should be given the choice of occupying that flat as her residence. [13]

**Disposition:** Disposed of

# Krishna Bhatacharjee vs. Sarathi Choudhury and Ors. (20.11.2015 - SC) : MANU/SC/ 1330/2015

**Relative Section:**

Protection of Women from Domestic Violence Act, 2005 - Section 2, Protection of Women from Domestic Violence Act, 2005 - Section 3, Protection of Women from Domestic Violence Act, 2005 - Section 8(1), Protection of Women from Domestic Violence Act, 2005 - Section 12, Protection of Women from Domestic Violence Act, 2005 - Section 12(1), Protection of Women from Domestic Violence Act, 2005 - Section 12(2), Protection of Women from Domestic Violence Act, 2005 - Section 18, Protection of Women from Domestic Violence Act, 2005 - Section 19, Protection of Women from Domestic Violence Act, 2005 - Section 20, Protection of Women from Domestic Violence Act, 2005 - Section 20(1), Protection of Women from Domestic Violence Act, 2005 - Section 21, Protection of Women from Domestic Violence Act, 2005 - Section 22, Protection of Women from Domestic Violence Act, 2005 - Section 23, Protection of Women from Domestic Violence Act, 2005 - Section 23(1), Protection of Women from Domestic Violence Act, 2005 - Section 28, Protection of Women from Domestic Violence Act, 2005 - Section 31, Protection of Women from Domestic Violence Act, 2005 - Section 32, Protection of Women from Domestic Violence Act, 2005 - Section 33, Protection of Women from Domestic Violence Act, 2005 - Section 36; Hindu Marriage Act, 1955 - Section 10, Hindu Marriage Act, 1955 - Section

10(2), Hindu Marriage Act, 1955 - Section 13(1A); Code of Criminal Procedure, 1973 (CrPC) - Section 468, Code of Criminal Procedure, 1973 (CrPC) - Section 498; Indian Penal Code, 1860 (IPC) - Section 406, Indian Penal Code, 1860 (IPC) - Section 498A; Protection of Women from Domestic Violence Rules, 2006 - Rule 15(6); Constitution of India - Article 14, Constitution of India - Article 15, Constitution of India - Article 21; Code of Civil Procedure, 1908 (CPC)

**Hon'bleJudges/Coram:** Dipak Misra and Prafulla C. Pant, JJ.

**Equivalent Citation:** 2015XII AD (S.C.) 101, 2016(157)AIC198, 2016(1)AJR545, 2016 (1) ALD(Crl.) 46 (SC), 2016 (92) ACC 443, (2016)1CALLT17(SC), IV(2015)CCR256(SC), 2016(1)CGLJ105, 2016(1) CLJ (SC)1, 2016CriLJ330, 2015(4)Crimes384(SC), III(2015)DMC823SC, 2016(1)ECrN 228, 2016GLH(1)1, 2016(1)HLR1, 2015/INSC/848, 2016(1)J.L.J.R.93, 2016(1)JCC31(SC), 2015(4)KLT999(SC), 2016-3-LW193, (2015) 4 MLJ(Crl) 623 (SC), 2016(III)MPJR1, 2016(1)N.C.C.239, 2016(1)PLJR158, 2016(1)RCR(Civil)151, 2016(1)RCR(Criminal)152, 2015(12)SCALE521, (2016)2SCC705, 2016 (3) SCJ 570, [2015]14SCR65, 2015(3)UC2229, 2016 (1) WLN 52 (SC)

**NumberofPagesintheOriginalJudgment: 14**

**Case Reference:**

Inderjit Singh Grewal vs. State of Punjab and Anr. MANU/SC/0988/ 2011; V.D. Bhanot vs. Savita Bhanot MANU/SC/0115/2012; Saraswathy vs. Babu MANU/SC/1193/2013; D. Velusamy vs. D. Patchaiammal MANU/ SC/0872/2010; Savitaben Somabhai Bhatiya vs. State of Gujarat and Ors. MANU/SC/0193/2005; Japani Sahoo vs. Chandra Sekhar Mohanty MANU/ SC/3080/2007; Noida Entrepreneurs Association vs. NOIDA and Ors. MANU/SC/0570/2011; Jeet Singh and Ors. vs. State of U.P. and Ors. MANU/SC/0436/1993; Hirachand Srinivas Managaonkar vs. Sunanda MANU/SC/0179/2001; Bai Mani vs. Jayantilal Dahyabhai MANU/GJ/ 0060/1979; Soundarammal vs. Sundara Mahalinga, Nadar MANU/TN/ 0232/1980; Pratibha Rani vs. Suraj Kumar and Anr. MANU/SC/0090/1985; Rashmi Kumar (Smt) vs. Mahesh Kumar Bhada MANU/SC/1052/1997; Raja Bhadur Singh v. Provident Fund Inspector and Ors. (1984) 4 SCC 222; State of Bihar vs. Deokaran Nenshi and Anr. MANU/SC/0469/1972

**Case Note:**

Family - Stridhan - Marriage between Appellant and Respondent No. 1 solemnised - Lived as husband and wife - Demand of dowry by husband and relatives - Appellant driven out of matrimonial home - Conciliation reached - With efflux of time - Husband filed petition for judicial separation - Granted - After judicial separation, Appellant filed Application - Section 12 of 2005 Act - Sought seizure of stridhan articles - Possession of husband - Learned Chief Judicial Magistrate held - No domestic relationship subsisted under 2005 Act - No relief could be granted - Criminal Appeal filed by Wife - Learned Additional Sessions Judge dismissed appeal - Held - Application barred by time - Revision preferred - High Court held - Proceedings under 2005 Act barred by limitation - Present Appeal - Whether the Appellant has ceased to be an "aggrieved person" because of the decree of judicial separation - Whether retention of stridhan by husband or any other family members is a continuing offence - Whether the application preferred by the wife was barred by limitation

**Facts:**

The marriage between the Appellant and the Respondent No. 1 was solemnised on 27.11.2005 and they lived as husband and wife. As the allegations proceed, there was demand of dowry by the husband including his relatives and, demands not being satisfied, the Appellant was driven out from the matrimonial home. However, due to intervention of the elderly people of the locality, there was some kind of conciliation as a consequence of which both the husband and the wife stayed in a rented house for two months. With the efflux of time, the husband filed a petition seeking judicial separation before the Family Court and eventually the said prayer was granted by the learned Judge, Family Court.

After the judicial separation, the Appellant filed an application Under Section 12 of the 2005 Act before the Child Development Protection Officer (CDPO), O/O the District Inspector, Social Welfare & Social Education, seeking necessary help as per the provisions contained in the 2005 Act. She sought seizure of Stridhan articles from the possession of the husband. The application which was made before the CDPO was forwarded by the said authority to the learned Chief Judicial Magistrate. The learned Magistrate taking into consideration the admitted fact that Respondent and the Appellant had entered into wedlock treated her as an "aggrieved person", but opined that no "domestic relationship" as defined Under Section 2(f) of the 2005 Act existed between the parties and, therefore, wife was not entitled to file the application Under Section 12 of the 2005 Act. The learned Magistrate came to hold that though the parties had not been divorced but the decree of judicial separation would be an impediment for entertaining the application and being of this view, he opined that no domestic relationship subsisted under the 2005 Act and hence, no relief could be granted.

The aggrieved wife preferred criminal appeal which has been decided by the learned Additional Sessions Judge holding, inter alia, that the object of the 2005 Act is primarily to give immediate relief to the victims; that as per the decision of this Court in Inderjit Singh Grewal v. State of Punjab that Section 468 of the Code of Criminal Procedure applies to the proceedings under the 2005 Act and, therefore, her application was barred by time. Being of this view, the appellate court dismissed the appeal.

On a revision being preferred, the High Court, after referring to Inderjit Singh Grewal v. State of Punjab, has stated that the wife had filed a criminal case Under Section 498(A) Indian Penal Code in 2006 and the husband had obtained a decree of judicial separation on 2008, and hence, the proceedings under 2005 Act was barred by limitation. That apart, it has also in a way expressed the view that the proceedings under 2005 Act was not maintainable. The present appeal has been filed against the said order.

**Held, while allowing the appeal**

The Court stated that the 2005 Act has been legislated, as its Preamble would reflect, to provide for more effective protection of the rights of the women guaranteed under the Constitution who are victims of violence of any kind occurring within the family and for matters connected therewith or incidental thereto. The 2005 Act is a detailed Act. The dictionary clause of the 2005 Act, which we shall advert to slightly at a later stage, is in a broader spectrum. The definition of "domestic violence" covers a range of violence which takes within its sweep "economic abuse" and the words "economic abuse", as the provision would show, has many a facet.[3]

Regard being had to the nature of the legislation, a more sensitive approach is expected from the courts where under the 2005 Act no relief can be granted, it should never be conceived of but, before throwing a petition at the threshold on the ground of maintainability, there has to be an apposite discussion and thorough deliberation on the issues raised. It should be borne in mind that helpless and hapless "aggrieved person" under the 2005 Act approaches the court under the compelling circumstances. It is the duty of the court to scrutinise the facts from all angles whether a plea advanced by the Respondent to nullify the grievance of the aggrieved person is really legally sound and correct. The principle "justice to the cause is equivalent to the salt of ocean" should be kept in mind. The court of law is bound to uphold the truth which sparkles when justice is done. Before throwing a petition at the threshold, it is obligatory to see that the person aggrieved under such a legislation is not faced with a situation of non-adjudication, for the 2005 Act as the Court has stated is a beneficial as well as assertively affirmative enactment for the realisation of the constitutional rights of women and to ensure that they do not become victims of any kind of domestic violence.[4]

There can be erroneous perception of law, but as the Court finds, neither the learned Magistrate nor the appellate court nor the High Court has made any effort to understand and appreciate the stand of the Appellant. Such type of cases and at such stage should not travel to this Court. The Court was compelled to say so as they were of the considered opinion that had the appellate court and the High Court been more vigilant, in all possibility, there could have been adjudication on merits. Be that as it may.[9]

The core issue that is requisite to be addressed is whether the Appellant has ceased to be an "aggrieved person" because of the decree of judicial separation. Once the decree of divorce is passed, the status of the parties becomes different, but that is not so when there is a decree for judicial separation. In view of judicial pronouncements, it is quite clear that there is a distinction between a decree for divorce and decree of judicial separation; in the former, there is a severance of status and the parties do not remain as husband and wife, whereas in the later, the relationship between husband and wife continues and the legal relationship continues as it has not been snapped. Thus understood, the finding recorded by the courts below which have been concurred by the High Court that the parties having been judicial separated, the Appellant wife has ceased to be an "aggrieved person" is wholly unsustainable.[18] and[22]

The Court has to see whether retention of stridhan by the husband or any other family members is a continuing offence or not. There can be no dispute that wife can file a suit for realization of the stridhan but it does not debar her to lodge a criminal complaint for criminal breach of trust. The Court must state that was the situation before the 2005 Act came into force. In the 2005 Act, the definition of "aggrieved person" clearly postulates about the status of any woman who has been subjected to domestic violence as defined Under Section 3 of the said Act. "Economic abuse" as it has been defined in Section 3(iv) of the said Act has a large canvass. Section 12, provides for procedure for obtaining orders of reliefs. It has been held in Inderjit Singh Grewal v. State of Punjab that Section 498 of the Code of Criminal Procedure applies to the said case under the 2005 Act as envisaged

Under Sections 28 and 32 of the said Act read with Rule 15(6) of the Protection of Women from Domestic Violence Rules, 2006. The Court is of the considered opinion that as long as the status of the aggrieved person remains and stridhan remains in the custody of the husband, the wife can always put forth her claim Under Section 12 of the 2005 Act.[31]

The Court is disposed to think so as the status between the parties is not severed because of the decree of dissolution of marriage. The concept of "continuing offence" gets attracted from the date of deprivation of stridhan, for neither the husband nor any other family members can have any right over the stridhan and they remain the custodians. For the purpose of the 2005 Act, she can submit an application to the Protection Officer for one or more of the reliefs under the 2005 Act. In the present case, the wife had submitted the application on 22.05.2010 and the said authority had forwarded the same on 01.06.2010. In the application, the wife had mentioned that the husband had stopped payment of monthly maintenance from January 2010 and, therefore, she had been compelled to file the application for stridhan. Regard being had to the said concept of "continuing offence" and the demands made, the Court is disposed to think that the application was not barred by limitation and the courts below as well as the High Court had fallen into a grave error by dismissing the application being barred by limitation.[31]

# CHAPTER TEN

# Hiral P. Harsora and Ors. vs. Kusum Narottamdas Harsora and Ors. (06.10.2016 - SC) : MANU/SC/1269/2016

**Relative Section:**

Protection of Women from Domestic Violence Act, 2005 - Section 2, Protection of Women from Domestic Violence Act, 2005 - Section 3, Protection of Women from Domestic Violence Act, 2005 - Section 8(1), Protection of Women from Domestic Violence Act, 2005 - Section 8(2), Protection of Women from Domestic Violence Act, 2005 - Section 8(3), Protection of Women from Domestic Violence Act, 2005 - Section 8(4), Protection of Women from Domestic Violence Act, 2005 - Section 9, Protection of Women from Domestic Violence Act, 2005 - Section 12(1), Protection of Women from Domestic Violence Act, 2005 - Section 12(2), Protection of Women from Domestic Violence Act, 2005 - Section 12(3), Protection of Women from Domestic Violence Act, 2005 - Section 17(2), Protection of Women from Domestic Violence Act, 2005 - Section 18, Protection of Women from Domestic Violence Act, 2005 - Section 19, Protection of Women from Domestic Violence Act, 2005 - Section 19(1), Protection of Women from Domestic Violence Act, 2005 - Section 20, Protection of Women from Domestic Violence Act, 2005 - Section 21, Protection of Women from Domestic Violence Act, 2005 - Section 22, Protection of Women from Domestic Violence Act, 2005 - Section 30, Protection of Women from Domestic Violence Act, 2005 - Section 31; Hindu Succession Act, 1956 - Section 6; Income Tax Act, 1961; East Punjab

Urban Rent Restriction Act 1949; Punjab Urban Rent Restriction Act, 1947; Government of India Act, 1935 [Repealed] - Section 93; Dowry Prohibition Act, 1961; Indian Penal Code, 1860 (IPC) - Section 498A; Delhi Special Police Establishment Act, 1946 - Section 6A; Prevention of Corruption Act, 1988; Central Excise Act, 1944 (Repealed); Calcutta Municipal Act, 1951 - Section 437; Andhra Pradesh Buildings (Lease, Rent and Eviction) Control Act, 1960 - Section 26; Andhra Pradesh Buildings (Lease, Rent and Eviction) Control Act, 1960 - Section 32; Madras Buildings (Lease and Rent Control) Act, 1949; Hyderabad Houses (Rent Eviction and Lease) Control Act, 1954; Delhi Rent Control Act, 1958 - Section 14(1); Sexual Harassment of Women at Workplace (Prevention, Prohibition and Redressal) Act, 2013; Hindu Women's Rights to Property Act, 1937 - Section 3; Code of Criminal Procedure, 1973 (CrPC) - Section 125; Constitution of India - Article 14, Constitution of India - Article 15, Constitution of India - Article 19(6), Constitution of India - Article 21; India (Provisional Constitution) Order, 1947 - Article 6

**Hon'bleJudges/Coram:** Kurian Joseph and Rohinton Fali Nariman, JJ.

**Equivalent Citation:** 2016(10)ADJ293, 2016(167)AIC5, AIR2016SC4774, 2017(2)ALD95, 2017 (1) ALD(Crl.) 923 (SC), 2016 (97) ACC 425, 2016ALLMR(Cri)4930, 2016 (119) ALR 462, 2017 (2) ALT (Crl.) 217(A.P.), 2016 6 AWC5830SC, 2016(6)BomCR505, 2017(1)CDR18(SC), 2016(5) CHN (SC) 86, 2017 CriL J509, 2016(4)Crimes91(SC), 120(1)CWN162, 233(2016)DLT154, III(2016)DMC438SC, 2016(4)ECrN 491, 2017(2)GLT1, 2016(3)HLR516, ILR2016(4)Kerala179, 2016/INSC/ 955, 2016(4)J.L.J.R.252, 2016(4)JCC2659, 2016(4)JKJ1[SC], 2018(1)JLJ529, 2016 (5) KHC 15, 2016(4)KLJ376, 2016(4)KLT268, 2017-3-LW28, 2017 (2)MhLj147, 2017(1)MLJ(Crl)348, 2017(2)MPLJ20, 2016(II)OLR995, 2016(4)PLJR348, 2016 (4)RCR (Civil) 750, 2016(4)RCR(Criminal)433, 2017(1)RLW689(SC), 2016(9)SCALE776, (2016)10SCC165, 2016 (9) SCJ 204, [2016]9SCR515, 2017(1)UC11, 2016 (4) WLN 19 (SC)

**NumberofPagesintheOriginalJudgment: 27**

**Case Reference:**

Kusum Lata Sharma v. State Crl.M.C. No. 75 of 2011; Shashikant Laxman Kale v. Union of India MANU/SC/0696/1990 : (1990) 2 SCR 441; A. Thangal Kunju Musaliar v. M. Venkitachalam Potti MANU/SC/0021/1955 : (1955) 2 SCR 1196 : AIR 1956 SC 246 : (1956) 29 ITR 349; State of West Bengal v. Union of India MANU/SC/0086/1962 : (1964) 1 SCR 371 : AIR

1963 SC 1241; Pannalal Binjraj v. Union of India MANU/SC/0020/1956 : 1957 SCR 233 : AIR 1957 SC 397 : (1957) 31 ITR 565; Harbilas Rai Bansal v. State of Punjab MANU/SC/0227/1996 : (1996) 1 SCC 1; Budhan Choudhry v. State of Bihar MANU/SC/0047/1954 : (1955) 1 SCR 1045 : AIR 1955 SC 191; Ram Krishna Dalmia v. Justice S.R. Tendolkar MANU/SC/0024/1958 : 1959 SCR 279 : AIR 1958 SC 538; Western U.P. Electric Power and Supply Co. Ltd. v. State of U.P. MANU/SC/0074/1969 : (1969) 1 SCC 817; Mohd. Hanif Quareshi v. State of Bihar MANU/SC/0027/1958 : 1959 SCR 629 : AIR 1958 SC 731; Sandhya Manoj Wankhade v. Manoj Bhimrao Wankhade MANU/SC/0081/2011 : (2011) 3 SCC 650; Indra Sarma v. V.K.V. Sarma MANU/SC/1230/2013 : (2013) 15 SCC 755; Andrahennedige Dinohamy v. Wijetunge Liyanapatabendige Balahamy MANU/PR/0116/1927 : (1928) 27 LW 678 : AIR 1927 PC 185; Badri Prasad v. Director of Consolidation MANU/SC/0004/1978 : (1978) 3 SCC 527; Tulsa v. Durghatiya MANU/SC/0424/2008 : (2008) 4 SCC 520; Badshah v. Urmila Badshah Godse and Anr. MANU/SC/1084/2013 : (2014) 1 SCC 188; Heydon Case (1584) 3 Co Rep 7a : 76 ER 637; State of U.P. v. Deoman Upadhyaya MANU/SC/0060/1960 : (1961) 1 SCR 14; Lachhman Dass v. State of Punjab MANU/SC/0032/1962 : (1963) 2 SCR 353; D.S. Nakara v. Union of India MANU/SC/0237/1982 : (1983) 1 SCC 305; In Re: Special Courts Bill MANU/SC/0039/1978 : (1979) 2 SCR 476; Maneka Gandhi v. Union of India MANU/SC/0133/1978 : (1978) 2 SCR 621; Rattan Arya and Ors. v. State of Tamil Nadu and Anr. MANU/SC/0550/1986 : (1986) 3 SCC 385; Subramanian Swamy v. CBI MANU/SC/0417/2014 : (2014) 8 SCC 682; State of Gujarat v. Shri Ambica Mills Ltd. MANU/SC/0092/1974 : (1974) 4 SCC 656 : 1974 SCC (L&S) 381 : (1974) 3 SCR 760; Union of India v. N.S. Ratnam MANU/SC/0806/2015 : (2015) 10 SCC 681; Roop Chand Adlakha v. DDA MANU/SC/0413/1988 : 1989 Supp (1) SCC 116 : 1989 SCC (L&S) 235 : (1989) 9 ATC 639; Corporation of Calcutta v. Calcutta Tramways Co. Ltd. MANU/SC/0043/1963 : [1964] 5 S.C.R. 25; Motor General Traders v. State of A.P. MANU/SC/0293/1983 : (1984) 1 SCC 222; Satyawati Sharma v. Union of India MANU/SC/1870/2008 : (2008) 5 SCC 287; R.M.D. Chamarbaugwalla v. Union of India MANU/SC/0020/1957 : AIR 1957 SC 628 : 1957 SCR 930; Lt. Col. Sawai Bhawani Singh v. State of Rajasthan MANU/SC/1103/1996 : (1996) 3 SCC 105; Cellular Operators Association of India v. TRAI MANU/SC/0551/2016 : (2016) 7 SCC 703; Owners of SS Kalibia v. Wilson (1910) 11 CLR 689 (Aust); Vacuum Oil Co. Pty. Ltd. v. Queensland (1934) 51 CLR 677 (Aust); R. v. Commonwealth Court of Conciliation and Arbitration, ex

p. Whybrow and Co. (1910) 11 CLR 1 (Aust); British Imperial Oil Co. Ltd. v. Federal Commr. of Taxation (1925) 35 CLR 422 (Aust); DTC v. Mazdoor Congress MANU/SC/0031/1991 : 1991 Supp (1) SCC 600 : 1991 SCC (L&S) 1213; B.R. Kapur v. State of T.N. MANU/SC/1659/2001 : (2001) 7 SCC 231

**Case Note:**

Constitution - Provision - Constitutional validity - Interpretation of expression - Section 2(q) of Protection of Women from Domestic Violence Act, 2005 - High Court held that provisions of "Respondent" in Section 2(q) of Act, 2005 was not to be read in isolation but had to be read as part of scheme of Act, 2005 - Further, complaint against daughter-in-law, daughters or sisters would be maintainable under provisions of Act, 2005 where they are co-Respondent/s in complaint against adult male person, who is or has been in domestic relationship with complainant and such co-respondent/s - Complaint under Act, 2005 would not be maintainable against daughter-in-law, sister-in-law or sister of complainant, if no complaint is filed against adult male person of family - Whether expression "adult male person" goes contrary to object of Act, 2005 - Whether rest of Act, 2005 can be implemented without two words i.e. "adult male"

**Facts:**

A duo of daughter and mother filed a complaint under the Protection of Women from Domestic Violence Act, 2005 against the brother/son, and his wife, and two sisters/daughters, alleging various acts of violence against them. The said complaint was withdrawn with liberty to file a fresh complaint. The same duo of mother and daughter filed two separate complaints against the same Respondents. An application was moved before the Metropolitan Magistrate for a discharge of Respondent Nos. 2 to 4 stating that as the complaint was made under Section 2(a) read with Section 2(q) of the Act, 2005, it can only be made against an adult male person and the three Respondents not being adult male persons were, therefore, required to be discharged. The Metropolitan Magistrate refused such discharge. In a petition filed against the said order, the High Court, discharged the three Respondents from the complaint. That order had since attained finality. The present proceedings arose because mother and daughter filed a petition, in which the constitutional validity of Section 2(q) was challenged. The High Court by the impugned judgment held that the provisions of "Respondent" in Section 2(q) of the Act, 2005 is not to be read in isolation but has to be read as a part of the scheme of the

Act, 2005 and particularly along with the definitions of "aggrieved person", "domestic relationship" and "shared household" in Clauses (a), (f) and (s) of Section 2 of the Act, 2005. If so read, the complaint alleging acts of domestic violence is maintainable not only against an adult male person who is son or brother, who is or has been in a domestic relationship with the aggrieved complainant-mother or sister, but the complaint can also be filed against a relative of the son or brother including wife of the son/wife of the brother and sisters of the male Respondent. In other words, the complaint against the daughter-in-law, daughters or sisters would be maintainable under the provisions of the Act, 2005 where they are co-Respondent/s in a complaint against an adult male person, who is or has been in a domestic relationship with the complainant and such co-respondent/s. A complaint under the Act, 2005 would not be maintainable against daughter-in-law, sister-in-law or sister of the complainant, if no complaint is filed against an adult male person of the family.

**Held, while disposing off the appeal:**

(i) A cursory reading of the statement of objects and reasons makes it clear that the phenomenon of domestic violence against women is widely prevalent and needs redressal. Whereas criminal law does offer some redressal, civil law does not address this phenomenon in its entirety. The idea therefore is to provide various innovative remedies in favour of women who suffer from domestic violence, against the perpetrators of such violence. [14]

(ii) It is not difficult to conceive of a non-adult 16 or 17 year old member of a household who can aid or abet the commission of acts of domestic violence, or who can evict or help in evicting or excluding from a shared household an aggrieved person. [24]

(iii) As per precedents, the microscopic difference between male and female, adult and non adult, regard being had to the object sought to be achieved by the Act, 2005 is neither real or substantial nor does it have any rational relation to the object of the legislation. In fact, as per the principle settled in the Subramanian Swamy v. CBI, the words "adult male person" are contrary to the object of affording protection to women who have suffered from domestic violence "of any kind". The words "adult male" before the word "person" in Section 2(q) were struck down, as these words discriminate between persons similarly situate, and far from being in tune with, are contrary to the object sought to be achieved by the Act, 2005. [36]

(iv) Having struck down the expression "adult male" in Section 2(q) of the Act, 2005 the rest of the Section is left intact and can be enforced to achieve the object of the legislation without the offending words. Under Section 2(q) of the Act, 2005 while defining 'Respondent', a proviso is provided only to carve out an exception to a situation of "Respondent" not being an adult male. Once 'adult male' are struck down, the proviso has no independent existence, having been rendered otiose. [40]

(v) The impugned judgment of the High Court was set aside and it was declared that the words "adult male" in Section 2(q) of the Act, 2005 will stand deleted since these words do not square with Article 14 of the Constitution of India. Consequently, the proviso to Section 2(q), being rendered otiose, also stood deleted. [46]

Disposition: Disposed of

# Kunapareddy vs. Kunapareddy Swarna Kumari and Ors. (18.04.2016 – SC) : MANU/ SC/0628/2016

**Relative Section:**

Protection of Women from Domestic Violence Act, 2005 - Section 9, Protection of Women from Domestic Violence Act, 2005 - Section 9(1), Protection of Women from Domestic Violence Act, 2005 - Section 9B, Protection of Women from Domestic Violence Act, 2005 - Section 12, Protection of Women from Domestic Violence Act, 2005 - Section 12(1), Protection of Women from Domestic Violence Act, 2005 - Section 13, Protection of Women from Domestic Violence Act, 2005 - Section 14, Protection of Women from Domestic Violence Act, 2005 - Section 15, Protection of Women from Domestic Violence Act, 2005 - Section 16, Protection of Women from Domestic Violence Act, 2005 - Section 17, Protection of Women from Domestic Violence Act, 2005 - Section 18, Protection of Women from Domestic Violence Act, 2005 - Section 19, Protection of Women from Domestic Violence Act, 2005 - Section 20, Protection of Women from Domestic Violence Act, 2005 - Section 21, Protection of Women from Domestic Violence Act, 2005 - Section 22, Protection of Women from Domestic Violence Act, 2005 - Section 23, Protection of Women from Domestic Violence Act, 2005 - Section 23(2), Protection of Women from Domestic Violence Act, 2005 - Section 24, Protection of Women from Domestic Violence Act, 2005 - Section 25, Protection of Women from Domestic Violence Act, 2005 - Section 26,

Protection of Women from Domestic Violence Act, 2005 - Section 27, Protection of Women from Domestic Violence Act, 2005 - Section 28, Protection of Women from Domestic Violence Act, 2005 - Section 28(1), Protection of Women from Domestic Violence Act, 2005 - Section 28(2), Protection of Women from Domestic Violence Act, 2005 - Section 29, Protection of Women from Domestic Violence Act, 2005 - Section 31, Protection of Women from Domestic Violence Act, 2005 - Section 37(2)(C); Hindu Marriage Act, 1955 - Section 23(2), Hindu Marriage Act, 1955 - Section 24; Code of Criminal Procedure, 1973 (CrPC) - Section 125, Code of Criminal Procedure, 1973 (CrPC) - Section 482; Indian Penal Code, 1860 (IPC) - Section 498A; Code of Civil Procedure, 1908 (CPC) - Order VI Rule 17; Constitution of India - Article 14, Constitution of India - Article 15, Constitution of India - Article 15(3), Constitution of India - Article 21, Constitution of India - Article 39, Constitution of India - Article 136

**Hon'bleJudges/Coram: A.K. Sikri and R.K. Agrawal, JJ.**

**Equivalent Citation:** 2016(163)AIC149, AIR2016SC2519, 2016(3)AJR550, 2016 (2) ALD(Crl.) 21 (SC), 2016ALLMR(Cri)3143,2016(117)ALR268,2016(3)BLJ185,2016(3)CCC 61,2016(2)CCC 254 , III (2016) CCR 207(SC),2016CriLJ2921, 2016(3)Crimes74(SC), 2016(2)Crimes277(SC), 2016(4)CTC314, II (2016) DMC 751 SC,2016(2)ECrN 722, 2016(3)HLR309, 2016/INSC/323, 2016(3)J.L.J.R.139, 2016 (3) JCC 1649,2017-1-LW (Crl)362, 2016(2)N.C.C.630,2016(3)PLJR242,2016(3)RCR(Civil)317,2016(3)RCR (Criminal) 315, 2016 (3)RL W2138(SC), 2016(5)SCALE703, (2016)11SCC774, 2016 (6) SCJ 34, [2016]2SCR608

**NumberofPagesintheOriginalJudgment: 12**

**Case Reference:**

Ramesh Chander Kaushal v. Venna Kaushal MANU/SC/0067/1978 : (1978) 4 SCC 70; S.R. Sukumar v. S. Sunaad Raghuram MANU/SC/0703/ 2015 : (2015) 9 SCC 609; U.P. Pollution Control Board v. Modi Distillery and Ors. MANU/SC/0912/1987 : (1987) 3 SCC 684

**Case Note:**

Civil - Amendment to petition/ complaint filed - Respondent No. 1-Wife of the Appellant - Filed a case against Appellant and his family - Sections 9-B & 37(2)(C) of Domestic Violence Act, 2005 - Various allegation levelled - Physical and mental harassment - Demand for dowry - Further alleged - Respondent No. 1 was driven out of the matrimonial home - On Appellant tendering an apology, they put up their family together - Things did not change - Respondent No. 1 filed a divorce petition - Made an application for interim maintenance as well - Also filed maintenance petition - Under Sections 23(2) and 24 - Hindu Marriage Act, 1955 - On receiving notice in DV petition - Family members of Appellant filed a petition - Section 482 of Code of Criminal Procedure - Quashing of proceedings in said DV Petition - Petition was allowed by High Court - Quashed the DV proceedings against family members of Appellant - Ground - There were no specific allegations against them - After DV petition transferred to Court of Judicial First Class Magistrate - Respondent No. 1 filed an application - Sought amendment of the Petition - Respondent No. 1 wanted to amend the prayer clause by incorporating some more prayers - Appellant opposed said application - Learned Trial Court allowed the amendment - Appellant raised objection - There was no power with Court to allow amendment - In Code of Criminal Procedure - Contention rejected by Trial Court - Premise that Section 26 of DV Act entitles a Civil Court, family court or a criminal court to grant any relief which is available to the complainant under Sections 18,19, 20, 21, & 22 of the said Act - Gives indication - Provisions of Code of Criminal Procedure would squarely apply - Court had power to allow amendment - Said order challenged by Appellant - Filed an appeal - Court of District and Sessions Judge set aside the order of Trial Court - Held - There was no specific provision for amendment of the complaint - Allowed the appeal of Appellant - Aggrieved, Respondent No. 1 filed a revision petition in High Court - High Court allowed the revision petition - Present appeal against order of High Court - Whether a court dealing with the petition/complaint filed under the provisions of the Domestic Violence Act, 2005 has power to allow amendment to the petition/complaint originally filed

**Facts:**

Respondent No. 1 herein, who is the wife of the Appellant, has filed a case against the Appellant and his family members before the Court of IInd Additional Judicial First Class Magistrate Under Sections 9-B & 37(2)(C) of the Domestic Violence Act, 2005 (the DV Act). The said petition now stands transferred to the Court of Judicial First Class Magistrate (Mobile Court). In this case, Respondent No. 1 has leveled various allegations against the Appellant and his family members inter alia alleging that the Appellant and his family members used to harass her physically as well as mentally and by also demanding dowry. It is further alleged that she was driven out from her matrimonial home in March, 2015 and initially she took shelter at her brother's house along with the children. Thereafter, on the

Appellant tendering an apology to Respondent No. 1 by coming to Eluru they put up their family together in one Gadam Ramakrishna's House, but the things did not change.

Respondent No. 1 has also filed a divorce petition before the Court of Senior Civil Judge, wherein she has made an application for interim maintenance as well. Thereafter, she also filed a maintenance petition Under Sections 23(2) and 24 of the Hindu Marriage Act, 1955 before the Court of Family Judge.

On receiving notice in DV Petition, family members of the Appellant filed a petition Under Section 482 Code of Criminal Procedure in the High Court for quashing the proceedings in the said DV Petition. This petition was allowed by the High Court thereby quashing the domestic violence proceedings against the family members of the Appellant on the ground that there were no specific allegations against them. After the DV Petition was transferred to the Court of Judicial First Class Magistrate, Respondent No. 1 filed an application seeking amendment of the petition. By way of the said amendment petition, Respondent No. 1 wanted to amend the prayer Clause by incorporating some more prayers.

The Appellant herein opposed the said application. However, the learned trial court after hearing both the parties allowed the amendment. The Appellant raised an objection that there was no power with the court to allow amendment of such a petition/complaint in the Code of Criminal Procedure, 1973 (the Code). This contention was rejected by the trial court on the premise that Section 26 of the DV Act, which entitles a civil court, a family court or a criminal court as well to grant any relief which is available to the complainant Under Sections 18, 19, 20, 21 & 22 of the said Act, gives an indication that the provisions of the Code of Civil Procedure would squarely apply and, therefore, the court had the power to allow amendment of the petition/complaint, more so, when it was necessary for the purpose of determining the real matter in controversy and to prevent multiplicity of the litigation.

The said order was challenged by the Appellant by filing an appeal before the Court of District and Sessions Judge who set aside the order of the Trial Court holding that there was no specific provision for amendment of the complaint and allowed the appeal of the Appellant. Aggrieved, Respondent No. 1 filed a revision petition in the High Court which has been allowed. The present appeal has been filed questioning the validity of the order of the High Court.

**Held, while dismissing the appeal**

1.No doubt Section 28 of the DV Act provides that all proceedings Under Sections 12, 19 to 23 as well as offences Under Section 31 are to be governed by the provisions of the Code. The instant petition, as noted above, is filed Under Section 9B and 37(2)(C) of the DV Act.[11]

2.The Court has already mentioned the prayers which were made by Respondent No. 1 in the original petition and prayer 'A' thereof relates to Section 9. However, in prayer 'B', the Respondent No. 1 also sought relief of grant of monthly maintenance to her as well as her children. This prayer falls within the ambit of Section 20 of the DV Act. In fact, prayer 'A" is covered by Section 18 which empowers the Magistrate to grant such a protection which is claimed by the Respondent No. 1. Therefore, the petition is essentially Under Sections 18 and 20 of the DV Act, though in the heading these provisions are not mentioned. However, that may not make any difference and, therefore, no issue was raised by the Appellant on this count. In respect of the petition filed Under Sections 18 and 20 of the DV Act, the proceedings are to be governed by the Code, as provided Under Section 28 of the DV Act. At the same time, it cannot be disputed that these proceedings are predominantly of civil nature.[12]

3.In fact, the very purpose of enacting the DV Act was to provide for a remedy which is an amalgamation of civil rights of the complainant i.e. aggrieved person. Intention was to protect women against violence of any kind, especially that occurring within the family as the civil law does not address this phenomenon in its entirety. It is treated as an offence Under Section 498A of the Indian Penal Code. The purpose of enacting the law was to provide a remedy in the civil law for the protection of women from being victims of domestic violence and to prevent the occurrence of domestic violence in the society. It is for this reason, that the Scheme of the Act provides that in the first instance, the order that would be passed by the Magistrate, on a complaint by the aggrieved person, would be of a civil nature and if the said order is violated, it assumes the character of criminality.[13]

4.Procedure for obtaining order of reliefs is stipulated in Chapter IV of the DV Act which comprises Sections 12 to 29. Under Section 12 an application can be made to the Magistrate by the aggrieved person or Protection Officer or any other person on behalf of the aggrieved person. The Magistrate is empowered, Under Section 18, to pass protection order. Section 19 of the DV Act authorizes the Magistrate to pass residence order which may include restraining the Respondent from dispossessing or disturbing the possession of the aggrieved person or directing the Respondent to remove himself from the shared household or even restraining the Respondent or his relatives from entering the portion of the shared household in which the aggrieved person resides etc. Monetary reliefs which can be granted by the Magistrate Under Section 20 of the DV Act include giving of the relief in respect of the loss of earnings, the medical expenses, the loss caused due to destruction, damage or removal of any property from the control of the aggrieved person and the maintenance for the aggrieved person as well as her children, if any.[14]

5.Custody can be decided by the Magistrate which was granted Under Section 21 of the DV Act. Section 22 empowers the Magistrate to grant compensation and damages for the injuries, including mental torture and emotional distress, caused by the domestic violence committed by the Appellant. All the aforesaid reliefs that can be granted by the Magistrate are of civil nature. Section 23 vests the Magistrate with the power to grant interim ex-parte orders. It is, thus, clear that various kinds of reliefs which can be obtained by the aggrieved person are of civil nature. At the same time, when there is a breach of such orders passed by the Magistrate, Section 31 terms such a breach to be a punishable offence.[14]

6.In the aforesaid scenario, merely because Section 28 of the DV Act provides for that the proceedings under some of the provisions including Sections 18 and 20 are essentially of civil nature. The Court took some aid and assistance from the nature of the proceedings filed Under Section 125 of the Code. Under the said provision as well, a woman and children can claim maintenance. At the same time these proceedings are treated essentially as of civil nature.[15]

7.The Court understood in this backdrop, it cannot be said that the Court dealing with the application under DV Act has no power and/or jurisdiction to allow the amendment of the said application. If the amendment becomes necessary in view of subsequent events [escalation of prices in the instant case] or to avoid multiplicity of litigation, Court will the have power to permit such an amendment. It is said that procedure is the handmaid of justice and is to come to the aid of the justice rather than defeating it. It is nobody's case that Respondent No. 1 was not entitled to file another application claiming the reliefs which she sought to include in the pending application by way of amendment. If that be so, the Court saw no reason, why the applicant be not allowed to incorporate this amendment in the pending application rather than filing a separate application. It is not that there is a complete ban/bar of amendment in the complaints in criminal Courts which are governed by the Code, though undoubtedly such power to allow the amendment has to be exercised sparingly and with caution under limited circumstances.[17]

8.What the Court is emphasising is that even in criminal cases governed by the Code, the Court is not powerless and may allow amendment in appropriate cases. One of the circumstances where such an amendment is to be allowed is to avoid the multiplicity of the proceedings. The argument of the learned Counsel for the Appellant, therefore, that there is no power of amendment has to be negated.[18]

9.In this context, provisions of Sub-section (2) of Section 28 of the DV Act gain significance. Whereas proceedings under certain Sections of the DV Act as specified in Sub-section (1) of Section 28 are to be governed by the Code, the Legislature at the same time incorporated the provisions like Sub-section (2) as well which empowers the Court to lay down its own procedure for disposal of the application Under Section 12 or Section 23(2) of the DV Act. This provision has been incorporated by the Legislature keeping a definite purpose in mind. Under Section 12, an application can be made to a Magistrate by an aggrieved person or a Protection Officer or any other person on behalf of the aggrieved person to claim one or more reliefs under the said Act. Section 23 deals with the power of the Magistrate to grant interim and ex-parte orders and Sub-section (2) of Section 23 is a special provision carved out in this behalf.[19]

10.The reliefs that can be granted by the final order or an by interim order, have already been pointed out above wherein it is noticed that most of these reliefs are of civil nature. If the power to amend the complaint/ application etc. is not read into the aforesaid provision, the very purpose which the Act attempts to sub-serve itself may be defeated in many cases.[20]

11.The Court, thus, was of the opinion that the amendment was rightly allowed by the Trial Court and there is no blemish in the impugned judgment of the High Court affirming the order of the Trial Court. This appeal is, thus, devoid of any merits and is, accordingly, dismissed with costs.[21]

Disposition: Appeal Dismissed

# CHAPTER TWELVE

# Manish Jain vs. Akanksha Jain (30.03.2017 - SC) : MANU /SC /0355 /2017

**Relative Section:**

Hindu Marriage Act, 1955 - Section 24; Protection of Women from Domestic Violence Act, 2005 - Section 23(2); Indian Penal Code, 1860 (IPC) - Section 406, Indian Penal Code, 1860 (IPC) - Section 498A; Code of Criminal Procedure, 1973 (CrPC) - Section 125, Code of Criminal Procedure, 1973 (CrPC) - Section 438

**Hon'bleJudges/Coram:** Kurian Joseph and R. Banumathi, JJ.

**Equivalent Citation:**2017(173)AIC88, AIR2017SC1640, 2017(4)ALD36,2017(3)ALLMR444, 2017(122) ALR 510, 2017(3)BomCR87,2017(2)CDR280(SC), 2017(2)CHN (SC) 91,2017(I)CLR(SC)1005, 121 (1)CWN 58,II(2017)DMC106SC,ILR2017(2)Kerala247,2017/INSC/300,2017/ INSC/297,2017(2)J.L.J.R.172,2017(2)JLJ 42,2017(2)KLJ640, 2017-3-LW884, 2017(I)OLR853, 2017(2)PLJR333,(2017)187PLR777,2017(2)RCR (Civil) 682,2017(2)RLW1641(SC), 2017(4)SCALE152, (2017)15SCC801, 2017 (3) SCJ 383, [2017]3SCR702, 2017 (1)UC711, 2017 (3) WLN 9 (SC)

**NumberofPagesintheOriginalJudgment: 6**

**Case Reference: nil**

**Case Note:**

Family - Grant of maintenance - Entitlement thereto - Section 24 of Hindu Marriage Act, 1955 - Additional District Judge declined to award maintenance pendente lite to Respondent-wife -High Court set aside that order - High Court granted interim maintenance to Respondent-wife - Hence, present appeal - Whether Respondent-wife was entitled to maintenance pendente lite - Whether amount awarded by High Court was on higher side

**Facts:**

Additional District Judge declined to award maintenance pendente lite to the Respondent-wife Under Section 24 of the Hindu Marriage Act, 1955. The High Court set aside that order. The High Court granted interim maintenance to the Respondent-wife at the rate of Rs. 60,000/- per month to be paid by the Appellant-husband. The said amount was fixed in addition to Rs. 10,000/- which the Appellant-husband was already paying by way of interim maintenance as per the order passed in criminal appeal Under Section 23(2) of the Protection of Women from Domestic Violence Act, 2005. Hence, the present appeal.

**Held, while allowing the appeal:**

(i) The Court exercises a wide discretion in the matter of granting alimony pendente lite but the discretion is judicial and neither arbitrary nor capricious. It is to be guided, on sound principles of matrimonial law and to be exercised within the ambit of the provisions of the Act and having regard to the object of the Act. The Court would not be in a position to judge the merits of the rival contentions of the parties when deciding an application for interim alimony and would not allow its discretion to be fettered by the nature of the allegations made by them and would not examine the merits of the case. Section 24 lays down that in arriving at the quantum of interim maintenance to be paid by one spouse to another, the Court must have regard to the Appellant's own income and the income of the Respondent. [11]

(ii) Section 24 of the HM Act empowers the Court in any proceeding under the Act, if it appears to the Court that either the wife or the husband, as the case may be, has no independent income sufficient for her or his support and the necessary expenses of the proceeding, it may, on the application of any one of them order the other party to pay to the Petitioner the expenses of the proceeding and monthly maintenance as may seem to be reasonable during the proceeding, having regard to also the income of both the applicant and the Respondent. [24]

(iii) At the time of claiming maintenance pendente lite when the Respondent-wife had no sufficient income capable of supporting herself, the High Court was justified in ordering maintenance. However, in our view, the maintenance amount of Rs. 60,000/- ordered by the High Court appeared to be on the higher side and in the interest of justice, the same was reduced to Rs. 25,000/- per month. The maintenance pendente lite of Rs. 25,000/- was to be paid to the Respondent-wife by the Appellant-husband. The order impugned was set aside. [16]

# CHAPTER THIRTEEN

# Vaishali Abhimanyu Joshi vs. Nanasaheb Gopal Joshi (09.05.2017 - SC) : MANU/ SC/0626/2017

**Relative Section:**

Protection of Women from Domestic Violence Act, 2005 - Section 2, Protection of Women from Domestic Violence Act, 2005 - Section 12, Protection of Women from Domestic Violence Act, 2005 - Section 13, Protection of Women from Domestic Violence Act, 2005 - Section 14, Protection of Women from Domestic Violence Act, 2005 - Section 15, Protection of Women from Domestic Violence Act, 2005 - Section 16, Protection of Women from Domestic Violence Act, 2005 - Section 17, Protection of Women from Domestic Violence Act, 2005 - Section 18, Protection of Women from Domestic Violence Act, 2005 - Section 19, Protection of Women from Domestic Violence Act, 2005 - Section 20, Protection of Women from Domestic Violence Act, 2005 - Section 21, Protection of Women from Domestic Violence Act, 2005 - Section 22, Protection of Women from Domestic Violence Act, 2005 - Section 23, Protection of Women from Domestic Violence Act, 2005 - Section 24, Protection of Women from Domestic Violence Act, 2005 - Section 25, Protection of Women from Domestic Violence Act, 2005 - Section 26, Protection of Women from Domestic Violence Act, 2005 - Section 26(1), Protection of Women from Domestic Thirleence Act, 2005 - Section 27, Protection of Women from Domestic Violence Act, 2005 - Section 28, Protection of Women from Domestic Violence Act, 2005 - Section 29;

Provincial Small Cause Courts Act, 1887 - Section 3, Provincial Small Cause Courts Act, 1887 - Section 5, Provincial Small Cause Courts Act, 1887 - Section 12, Provincial Small Cause Courts Act, 1887 - Section 15, Provincial Small Cause Courts Act, 1887 - Section 18, Provincial Small Cause Courts Act, 1887 - Section 19, Provincial Small Cause Courts Act, 1887 - Section 20, Provincial Small Cause Courts Act, 1887 - Section 21, Provincial Small Cause Courts Act, 1887 - Section 22, Provincial Small Cause Courts Act, 1887 - Section 26, Provincial Small Cause Courts Act, 1887 - Section 26(1), Provincial Small Cause Courts Act, 1887 - Section 26(2), Provincial Small Cause Courts Act, 1887 - Section 26A, Provincial Small Cause Courts Act, 1887 - Section 26B, Provincial Small Cause Courts Act, 1887 - Section 26C; Bombay Rents, Hotel and Lodging House Rates Control Act, 1947 [Repealed Act];Bombay Government Premises (Eviction) Act, 1955;Bombay Provincial Municipal Corporations Act, 1919;Maharashtra Housing and Area Development Act, 1976;Code of Civil Procedure, 1908 (CPC) - Section 9A; Indian Penal Code, 1860 (IPC) - Section 498A; Code of Civil Procedure, 1908 (CPC) - Order VIII Rule 6, Code of Civil Procedure, 1908 (CPC) - Order VIII Rule 6A, Code of Civil Procedure, 1908 (CPC) - Order L; Constitution of India - Article 14, Constitution of India - Article 15, Constitution of India - Article 21

**Hon'bleJudges/Coram:** A.K. Sikri and Ashok Bhushan, JJ.

**Equivalent Citation:**

2017(4)ABR634, 2017(176)AIC235, AIR2017SC2926, 2017(5)ALD65, 2017 (100) ACC 680, 2017 (6) ALL MR 404, 2017 (4) CCC 401 , 2017(II)CLR(SC)403, III(2017)DMC245SC, 2018(3)ECrN 753, 2017(3)HLR456, 2017/INSC/459, 2017(3)JCC1710, 2017(6)JKJ30[SC], 2017-5-LW842, 2017(2)RCR(Civil)1021, 2017 (2) RCR (Criminal)957, 2017(6)SCALE478, (2017)14SCC373, [2017]5SCR488

**NumberofPagesintheOriginalJudgment: 14**

**Case Reference:**

Kunapareddy alias Nookala Shanka Balaji v. Kunapareddy Swarna Kumari and Anr. MANU/SC/0628/2016 : (2016) 11 SCC 774; Union of India and Anr. v. G.M. Kokil and Ors. MANU/SC/0210/1984 : 1984 (Supp) SCC 196; Ambreen Akhoon v. Aditya Aurn Paudwal and Ors. Writ Petition No. 5648 of 2015; Allahabad Bank v. Canara Bank MANU/SC/0262/2000 : 2000 (4) SCC 406; Solidaire India Ltd. v. Fair Growth Financial Services Ltd. and Ors. MANU/SC/0009/2001 : 2001 (3) SCC 71; Bank of India v. Ketan Parekh MANU/SC/2700/2008 : 2008 (8) SCC 148; Hiral P. Harsora and Ors. v. Kusum Narottamdas Harsora and Ors. MANU/SC/1269/2016 : 2016 (10) SCC 165

**Case Note:**

Property - Right of residence - Counter claim - Entertaining thereof - Small Cause Courts - Section 19 of Protection of Women from Domestic Violence Act, 2005 (Act, 2005) and Sections 15 and 26 of Provincial Small Cause Courts Act, 1887 (Act, 1887) - Respondent filed suit in Small Causes Court - Respondent/Plaintiff filed application claiming that declaration sought by Appellant in suit was not maintainable - Hence, preliminary issue be framed - Application was objected by Appellant - Appellant claimed that since she had been subjected to domestic violence she was entitled for reliefs sought by way of counter claim as provided in Act, 2005 - Contended that reliefs sought by way of counter claim were not barred as per Section 15 of Act, 1887 - Trial Court framed preliminary issue "as to whether Court has jurisdiction to entertain counter claim" - Judge held that Court had no jurisdiction to entertain counter claim - Revision was filed against order passed by Small Causes Court before District Judge - District Judge rejected revision - Appellant filed petition which was dismissed by judgment - High Court held that Small Causes Court constituted under Act, 1887 cannot entertain and try counter claim - Hence, present appeal - Whether Appellant's counter claim seeking right of residence under Section 19 of Act, 2005 can be entertained in suit filed against her under Section 26 of Act, 1887 seeking mandatory injunction directing her to stop using suit flat and to remove her belongings therefrom - Whether provisions of Act, 1887 bar entertainment of such counter claim

**Facts:**

The Appellant got married with son of the Respondent. The Appellant started residing in the suit flat alongwith her husband. The flat was allotted to the Respondent by the Society. A daughter was born from their wedlock. The husband of Appellant left her at the suit flat and shifted to live with his parent. The Respondent along with his wife had been residing in another flat nearby. The Appellant was treated with cruelty by her husband and other members of the family. A suit for divorce on the basis of cruelty was filed by the Appellant against her husband. A notice was sent on behalf of the Respondent to the Appellant revoking the gratuitous licence and asking the Appellant to stop the use and occupation of the suit flat. The Appellant replied the notice. The Respondent filed suit in the Small Causes Court. The Appellant filed a written statement in the suit pleading that she was residing in the suit flat along with her husband and daughter. Her husband who was also residing along with her left her to live with the Respondent. It was pleaded that suit flat was intended to be used by the joint family as a joint family property and although the agreement of purchase of the suit flat bore the name of the Respondent, the suit flat was used as joint family property. The allegation that Respondent was the sole owner of the flat was denied. The Respondent/Plaintiff filed an application Under Section 9A (Maharashtra Amendment) of the Code of Civil Procedure, 1908. In the application, the Respondent claimed that declaration sought by the Appellant in the suit was not maintainable, hence, a preliminary issue Under Section 9A of Code of Civil Procedure be framed. The application was objected by the Appellant. The Appellant claimed that since she had been subjected to domestic violence she was entitled for the reliefs sought by way of counter claim as provided in the Protection of Women from Domestic Violence Act, 2005 (Act, 2005). It was contended that the reliefs sought by way of counter claim were not barred as per Section 15 of the Provincial Small Cause Courts Act, 1887 (Act, 1887). The Trial Court framed preliminary issue "as to whether the Court has jurisdiction to entertain the counter claim". Judge Small Causes Court held that Court had no jurisdiction to entertain the counter claim. Revision was filed against the order passed by the Small Causes Court before the District Judge. The District Judge rejected the revision which order was challenged by the Appellant by means of writ petition which was dismissed by judgment. The High Court held that in view of the express language in Section 15 as also the Second Schedule of Act, 1887, the Small Causes Court constituted under Act, 1887 cannot entertain and try the counter claim. Aggrieved by the order of the High Court, the Appellant filed the present appeal.

**Held:**

(i) The Provincial Small Cause Courts Act, 1887 was enacted to consolidate and amend the law relating to Courts of Small Causes established beyond the Presidency-towns. The Protection of Women from Domestic Violence Act, 2005 has been enacted to provide for more effective protection of the rights of women guaranteed under the Constitution who are victims of violence of any kind occurring within the family and for matters connected therewith or incidental thereto. Act, 2005 was enacted by the Parliament to give effect to various international conventions. There cannot be any dispute that proceeding before the Judge, Small Causes Court is a legal proceeding and the Judge, Small Causes Court is a civil court. On the strength of Section 26 any relief available Under Section 18 to 22 of Act, 2005, thus, can also be sought by the aggrieved person. [13],[17] and[20]

(ii) "Notwithstanding anything contained elsewhere in this Act" as used in Section 26(1) of Act, 1887 are words of expression of the widest amplitude engulfing the contrary provisions contained in the Act. The suit in question was filed by the Plaintiff for enforcement of his right as a licensor after allegedly terminating the gratuitous licence of the Appellant. On a plain reading Item No. 11 of Schedule II covers determination or enforcement of any such right or interest in immovable property. But by virtue of Section 26 Sub-section (1) as applicable in State of Maharashtra, Item No. 11 of Schedule 2 has to give way to Section 26(1) and a suit between licensor and licensee which is virtually a suit for recovery of immovable property is fully maintainable in Judge, Small Causes Court that is why the suit was instituted by the Plaintiff in the Judge, Small Causes Court claiming the right and interest in the immovable property. [29]

(iii) When the suit filed by the Plaintiff for determination or enforcement of his right as a licensor can be taken cognizance by Judge, Small Causes Court the relief claimed by the Appellant in the Court of Small Causes within the meaning of Section 26 of Act. 2005 can be considered by the Judge, Small Causes Court. In facts of the present case, the bar and embargo under Item No. 11 of Schedule II read with Section 15 of Act, 1887 stand whittled down and engulfed by virtue of Section 26 Sub-section (1) as applicable in the State. [30]

(iv) Section 26 of the Act, 2005 has to be interpreted in a manner to effectuate the very purpose and object of the Act. Unless the determination of claim by an aggrieved person seeking any order as contemplated by Act, 2005 is expressly barred from consideration by a civil court, this Court shall be loath to read in bar in consideration of any such claim in any legal proceeding before the civil court. When the proceeding initiated by Plaintiff in the Judge, Small Causes Court alleged termination of gratuitous licence of the Appellant and prays for restraining the Appellant from using the suit flat and permit the Plaintiff to enter and use the flat, the right of residence as claimed by the Appellant is inter-connected with such determination and refusal of consideration of claim of the Appellant as raised in her counter claim shall be nothing but denying consideration of claim as contemplated by Section 26 of the Act, 2005 which shall lead to multiplicity of proceeding, which can not be the object and purpose of Act, 2005. The counter claim filed by the Appellant before Judge, Small Causes Court was fully entertainable and courts below committed error in refusing to consider such claim. The judgment of the High Court and order of Small Causes Court as well as judgment of the District Judge was set aside. [36], [37] and[39]

**Disposition:** Appeal Allowed

# Manmohan Attavar vs. Neelam Manmohan Attavar (14.07.2017 - SC) : MANU/ SC/0808/2017

**Relative Section:**

Protection of Women From Domestic Violence Act, 2005 - Section 2, Protection of Women From Domestic Violence Act, 2005 - Section 12, Protection of Women From Domestic Violence Act, 2005 - Section 12(1), Protection of Women From Domestic Violence Act, 2005 - Section 29; Code of Criminal Procedure, 1973 (CrPC) - Section 327, Code of Criminal Procedure, 1973 (CrPC) - Section 407, Code of Criminal Procedure, 1973 (CrPC) - Section 410, Code of Criminal Procedure, 1973 (CrPC) - Section 482; Constitution of India - Article 226, Constitution of India - Article 227

**Hon'bleJudges/Coram:** Rohinton Fali Nariman and Sanjay Kishan Kaul, JJ.

**Equivalent Citation:** 2017(179)AIC267, AIR2017SC3345, 2017(4)AJR660, 2017(5)ALD120, 2017 (101) ACC 943, 2017(3)BLJ169, 2017(3)CDR520(SC), 2017CriLJ4315, 2017(4)Crimes70(SC), II(2017) DMC 806 SC, 2018(3)ECrN 583, 2017/INSC/618, 2017(3)JCC1940, 2017(5)JKJ21[SC], 2017(4)KCCR3361, 2018-1-LW158, 2018(1)MhLj839, 2018(1)MPLJ252, (2017)188PLR687, 2017(3)RCR(Civil)916, 2017(3) RCR (Criminal)686, 2017(4)RLW3022(SC), 2017(7)SCALE710, (2017)8SCC550, 2017 (9) SCJ 295, [2017]6SCR356, 2017(3)UC1801, (2017)6WBLR(SC)22

**NumberofPagesintheOriginalJudgment:** 7

**Case Reference:** .R. Antulay v. Ram Naik MANU/SC/0002/1988 : (1988) 2 SCC 602

**Case Note:**

Family - Withdrawal of proceedings - Occupancy right of premises - Section 12 of Protection of Women from Domestic Violence Act, 2005 - Application of interim relief was rejected - High Court withdraw all proceedings from Trial Court - Ex parte order was passed - Respondent was granted permission to occupy premises of Appellant - Hence, present appeal by Appellant - Whether interim order permitting Respondent to occupy premises of Appellant was justified - Whether High Court order of withdrawal of proceedings pending before Trial Court was maintainable.

**Facts:**

The Respondent was in a relationship with the Appellant despite the fact that he was married and had a living spouse. The Respondent initiated proceedings under Section 12 of The Protection of Women from Domestic Violence Act, 2005. The application was transferred on the request of the Respondent from one court to another. The application of interim relief was rejected. The Respondent again sought a transfer from that court and the appeal was transferred to another Court. The Respondent was once again aggrieved by the conduct of the proceedings filed a complaint to the High Court. The application was not maintainable. High Court by an ex parte order stayed all further proceedings and permitted the Respondent to occupy the premises of the Appellant. Hence, present appeal by the Appellant.

**Held, while allowing the appeals:**

(i) The ex parte order permitting the Respondent to occupy the premises of the Appellant was set aside on the ground that the Respondent had never stayed with the Appellant in the premises. In order for the Respondent to succeed, it was necessary that the two parties had lived in a domestic relationship in the household. As the Appellant was Christian there could be no question of marrying the Respondent by applying kumkum that to when the wife of the Appellant was alive. [17]

(ii) The order of High Court of withdrawing the appeals from Trial Court was set aside on the ground of insufficient reasons. There was not only absence of the reason for the same but it would also result in the deprivation of valuable rights of the Appellant against the order of an Appellate authority. [23] and[26]

**Disposition:** Appeal Allowed

# CHAPTER FIFTEEN

# Ajay Kumar vs. Lata and Ors. (08.04.2019 – SC) : MANU /SC/0651/2019

**Relative Section:**

Protection of Women from Domestic Violence Act, 2005 - Section 2, Protection of Women from Domestic Violence Act, 2005 - Section 12, Protection of Women from Domestic Violence Act, 2005 - Section 12(1), Protection of Women from Domestic Violence Act, 2005 - Section 20(1); Code of Criminal Procedure, 1973 (CrPC) - Section 125; Constitution of India - Article 136

**Hon'bleJudges/Coram:** Dr. D.Y. Chandrachud and Hemant Gupta, JJ.

**Equivalent Citation:** 2021(1)ACR254, 2019(202)AIC101, AIR2019SC2600, 2020 (1) ALD(Crl.) 218 (SC), 2019 (109) ACC 217, 2019(4)BLJ73, 2019 (2) CCC 452 , 2019(3)CGLJ220, 2019(3)CivilCC(S.C.), 2019 CriLJ3344, 2019(2)Crimes359(SC), 260(2019)DLT35, II(2019)DMC241SC, 2019(2)HLR411, 2019/INSC/473, 2019(3)JCC1946, 2019(2)JKJ123[SC], 2019(2)JLJ595, 2019 (3) KHC 164, 2019(2)KLJ963, 2019(II)OLR167, 2019(2)RCR(Criminal)1016, 2019(2)RLW1671(SC), 2019(7)SCALE193, (2019)15SCC352, [2019]6SCR283

**NumberofPagesintheOriginalJudgment: 6**

**Case Reference: nil**

**Case Note:**

Family - Payment of maintenance - Issuance of direction - Sections 12, 20 2(q) and 2(s) of Protection of Women from Domestic Violence Act, 2005 - Present appeal arose from a judgment of a learned Single Judge of

High Court dismissing a petition against judgment of Additional Sessions Judge, confirming an interim order for award of maintenance to first Respondent and her minor child under the provisions of Act, 2005 - Whether impugned directions for payment of maintenance were liable to be set aside.

**Facts:**

The first Respondent was married to Vijay Kumar Jindal on 12 December 2019. They have two children. The first Respondent filed a petition under Section 12 of the Act for the purpose of seeking an award of maintenance. The complaint contains a recital of the fact that after her marriage, the complainant and her spouse resided at a house which constitutes ancestral Hindu Joint Family Property. She and her husband resided on the ground floor of the residential accommodation. The Appellant and the deceased spouse of the first Respondent jointly carried on a business of a kiryana store at Panipat from which, it has been alleged, each had an income of about Rs. 30,000 per month. The complaint alleges that, at the death of Vijay Kumar, the first Respondent was pregnant and that she gave birth to a child on 31 January 2013. The travails of the first Respondent are alleged to have commenced after the death of her spouse and she was not permitted to reside in her matrimonial home. The learned Trial Judge by an order granted monthly maintenance in the amount of Rs. 4,000 to the first Respondent and Rs. 2,000 to the second Respondent. The award of maintenance was directed against the Appellant who was carrying on the above business together with the deceased spouse of the first Respondent. This order of the Judicial Magistrate, was confirmed by the Additional Sessions Judge. The High Court, in a petition filed by the Appellant, affirmed the view. Hence, present proceedings.

**Held, while disposing of the appeal**

1. The submission which has been urged on behalf of the Appellant is that there was no basis under the provisions of the Act to fasten liability on the Appellant, who is the brother of the deceased spouse of the first Respondent. Learned Counsel submitted that the sole basis on which liability has been fastened is that the Appellant and his deceased brother carried on a joint business. This cannot furnish any lawful basis to direct the Appellant to meet the award of maintenance. [7]

2. Section 12(1) provides that an aggrieved person may present an application to the Magistrate seeking one or more reliefs under the Act. Under the provisions of Section 20(1), the Magistrate while dealing with

an application Under Sub-section (1) of Section 12 is empowered to direct the Respondent(s) to pay monetary relief to meet the expenses incurred and losses suffered by the aggrieved person and any child of the aggrieved person as a result of domestic violence. This may include but is not limited to an order for maintenance of the aggrieved person as well as her children, if any, including an order under or in addition to an order for maintenance under Section 125 of CrPC or any other law for the time being in force. [9]

3. The substantive part of Section 2(q) indicates that the expression "Respondent" means any adult male person who is, or has been, in a domestic relationship with the aggrieved person and against whom relief has been sought. The proviso indicates that both, an aggrieved wife or a female living in a relationship in the nature of marriage may also file a complaint against a relative of the husband or the male partner, as the case may be. [11]

4. Section 2(f) defines the expression 'domestic relationship' to mean a relationship where two persons live or have lived together at any point of time in a shared household when they are related by consanguinity, marriage or through a relationship in the nature of marriage, adoption or are members living together as a joint family. [13]

5. The expression "shared household" is defined in Section 2(s) as a household where the person aggrieved lives or at any stage has lived in a domestic relationship either singly or along with the Respondent and includes such a house hold whether owned or tenanted either jointly by the aggrieved person and the Respondent, or owned or tenanted by either of them in respect of which either the aggrieved person or the Respondent or both jointly or singly have any right, title, interest or equity and includes such a household which may belong to the joint family of which the Respondent is a member, irrespective of whether the Respondent or the aggrieved person has any right, title or interest in the shared household. [14]

6. All these definitions indicate the width and amplitude of the intent of Parliament in creating both an obligation and a remedy in the terms of the enactment. [15]

7. At the present stage, there are sufficient averments in the complaint to sustain the order for the award of interim maintenance. Paragraph 10 of the complaint prima facie indicates that, the case of the complainants is that the house where the first Respondent and her spouse resided, belong to a joint family. The Appellant and his brother (who was the spouse of

the first Respondent and father of the second Respondent) carried on a joint business. The Appellant resided in the same household. Ultimately, whether the requirements of Section 2(f); Section 2(q); and Section 2(s) are fulfilled is a matter of evidence which will be adjudicated upon at the trial. At this stage, for the purpose of an interim order for maintenance, there was material which justifies the issuance of a direction in regard to the payment of maintenance. [18]

8. The Appeal is, accordingly, disposed of. [21]

**Ratio Decidendi:** An aggrieved wife or a female living in a relationship in nature of marriage is entitled to maintenance, against a relative of the husband or the male partner

**Disposition:** Disposed of

# Vasant Ganpat Padave (D) by L.Rs. and Ors. vs. Anant Mahadev Sawant (D) through L.Rs. and Ors. (18.09.2019 - SC) : MANU/SC/1285/2019

**Relative Section:**

Bombay Tenancy And Agricultural Lands Act 1948 - Section 2(18), Bombay Tenancy And Agricultural Lands Act 1948 - Section 2(6), Bombay Tenancy And Agricultural Lands Act 1948 - Section 2(8), Bombay Tenancy And Agricultural Lands Act 1948 - Section 4, Bombay Tenancy And Agricultural Lands Act 1948 - Section 4B, Bombay Tenancy And Agricultural Lands Act 1948 - Section 14, Bombay Tenancy And Agricultural Lands Act 1948 - Section 14(1), Bombay Tenancy And Agricultural Lands Act 1948 - Section 15, Bombay Tenancy And Agricultural Lands Act 1948 - Section 29, Bombay Tenancy And Agricultural Lands Act 1948 - Section 29(1), Bombay Tenancy And Agricultural Lands Act 1948 - Section 30, Bombay Tenancy And Agricultural Lands Act 1948 - Section 31, Bombay Tenancy And Agricultural Lands Act 1948 - Section 31A, Bombay Tenancy And Agricultural Lands Act 1948 - Section 31B, Bombay Tenancy And Agricultural Lands Act 1948 - Section 31C, Bombay Tenancy And Agricultural Lands Act 1948 - Section 31D, Bombay Tenancy And Agricultural Lands Act 1948 - Section 31(1), Bombay Tenancy And

Agricultural Lands Act 1948 - Section 31(2), Bombay Tenancy And
Agricultural Lands Act 1948 - Section 31(3), Bombay Tenancy And
Agricultural Lands Act 1948 - Section 32, Bombay Tenancy And
Agricultural Lands Act 1948 - Section 32(1), Bombay Tenancy And
Agricultural Lands Act 1948 - Section 32A, Bombay Tenancy And
Agricultural Lands Act 1948 - Section 32B, Bombay Tenancy And
Agricultural Lands Act 1948 - Section 32C, Bombay Tenancy And
Agricultural Lands Act 1948 - Section 32D, Bombay Tenancy And
Agricultural Lands Act 1948 - Section 32E, Bombay Tenancy And
Agricultural Lands Act 1948 - Section 32F, Bombay Tenancy And
Agricultural Lands Act 1948 - Section 32G, Bombay Tenancy And
Agricultural Lands Act 1948 - Section 32H, Bombay Tenancy And
Agricultural Lands Act 1948 - Section 32I, Bombay Tenancy And
Agricultural Lands Act 1948 - Section 32J, Bombay Tenancy And
Agricultural Lands Act 1948 - Section 32K, Bombay Tenancy And
Agricultural Lands Act 1948 - Section 32L, Bombay Tenancy And
Agricultural Lands Act 1948 - Section 32M, Bombay Tenancy And
Agricultural Lands Act 1948 - Section 32N, Bombay Tenancy And
Agricultural Lands Act 1948 - Section 32O, Bombay Tenancy And
Agricultural Lands Act 1948 - Section 32P, Bombay Tenancy And
Agricultural Lands Act 1948 - Section 32P(2), Bombay Tenancy And
Agricultural Lands Act 1948 - Section 32Q, Bombay Tenancy And
Agricultural Lands Act 1948 - Section 32R, Bombay Tenancy And
Agricultural Lands Act 1948 - Section 32(1A), Bombay Tenancy And
Agricultural Lands Act 1948 - Section 32F(1), Bombay Tenancy And
Agricultural Lands Act 1948 - Section 32F(1A), Bombay Tenancy And
Agricultural Lands Act 1948 - Section 32G(1), Bombay Tenancy And
Agricultural Lands Act 1948 - Section 32P(1), Bombay Tenancy And
Agricultural Lands Act 1948 - Section 32G(5), Bombay Tenancy And
Agricultural Lands Act 1948 - Section 33C, Bombay Tenancy And
Agricultural Lands Act 1948 - Section 63, Bombay Tenancy And
Agricultural Lands Act 1948 - Section 74, Bombay Tenancy And
Agricultural Lands Act 1948 - Section 431D; Central Sales Tax Act, 1956
- Section 8, Central Sales Tax Act, 1956 - Section 8(1), Central Sales Tax
Act, 1956 - Section 8(2), Central Sales Tax Act, 1956 - Section 10A; Code of
Criminal Procedure, 1973 (CrPC) - Section 423(1); Constitution of India -
Article 14, Constitution of India - Article 19, Constitution of India - Article
31A, Constitution of India - Article 31A(1); Haryana Urban (control Of

Rent And Eviction) Act 1973 - Section 13(3); Income Tax Act, 1961 - Section 40(a), Income Tax Act, 1961 - Section 40(c), Income Tax Act, 1961 - Section 52, Income Tax Act, 1961 - Section 52(2); Indian Income-tax Act, 1922 - Section 16(3), Indian Income-tax Act, 1922 - Section 24(2), Indian Income-tax Act, 1922 - Section 33B; Indian Income-tax Act, 1922 - Section 33B(2); Indian Income-tax Act, 1922 - Section 33B(4); Land Acquisition Act, 1894 - Section 18, Land Acquisition Act, 1894 - Section 28A; Opium (Madhya Bharat Amendment) Act, 1955 - Section 11, Opium (Madhya Bharat Amendment) Act, 1955 - Section 11(d); Protection Of Women From Domestic Violence Act, 2005 - Section 2(q); Representation Of The People Act, 1951 - Section 99(1); Tamil Nadu Buildings (lease And Rent Control) Act, 1960 - Section 10(3); Uttar Pradesh Zamindari Abolition And Land Reforms Act, 1950 - Section 9; Tenancy and Agricultural Lands Laws (Amendment) Act, 1969

**Hon'bleJudges/Coram:** Rohinton Fali Nariman, R. Subhash Reddy and Surya Kant, JJ.

**Equivalent Citation:** 2020(2)BomCR563, 2019/INSC/1050, 2019(12)SCALE579, (2019)19SCC577, [2019]15SCR569

**NumberofPagesintheOriginalJudgment:** 37

**Case Reference:**

Vasant Ganpat Padave (D) by L.Rs. and Ors. v. Anant Mahadev Sawant (Dead) thru. L.Rs. and Ors. MANU/SC/1490/2018; Appa Narsappa Magdum (D)Thr. Lrs v. Akubai Ganapati Nimbalkar and Ors MANU/SC/0375/1999; Sudam Ganpat Kutwal P.A. Holder of Shankar Sitaram Bhosle v. Shevantabai Tukaram Gulumkar (dead) by LR Maruti Shankar Pachpute MANU/SC/8422/2006; Tukaram Maruti Chavan v. Maruti Narayan Chavan (Dead) by LRs. and Ors. MANU/SC/4167/2008; Sri Ram Ram Narain Medhi v. The State of Bombay MANU/SC/0132/1958; Amrit Bhikaji Kale and Ors. v. Kashinath Janardhan and Anr. MANU/SC/0355/1983; Musamia Imam Haider Bax Razvi v. Rabari Govindbhai Ratnabhai and Ors. MANU/SC/0393/1968; Tirath Singh v. Bachittar Singh and Ors. MANU/SC/0048/1955; Ramaswamy Nadar v. The State of Madras MANU/SC/0048/1957; State of Madhya Pradesh v. Azad Bharat Finance Co. and Anr. MANU/SC/0089/1966; Bhudan Singh and Anr. v. Nabi Bux and Anr. MANU/SC/0353/1969; Commissioner of Income Tax, Central, Calcutta v. National Taj Traders MANU/SC/0310/1979; K.P. Varghese v. Income Tax Officer, Ernakulam and Anr. MANU/SC/0300/1981; Commissioner of Income Tax, Bangalore v. J.H. Gotla, Yadagiri MANU/SC/0126/1985; Thiru Manickam and Co. v. The State of Tamil Nadu MANU/SC/0427/1976; State of Tamil Nadu v. Kodaikanal Motor Union (P) Ltd. MANU/SC/0127/1986; Hameedia Hardware Stores, represented by its partner S. Peer Mohammed v. B. Mohan Lal Sowcar MANU/SC/0180/1988; Surjit Singh Kalra v. Union of India (UOI) and Anr. MANU/SC/0529/1991; Sirajul Haq Khan and Ors. v. The Sunni Central Board of Waqf, U.P. and Ors. MANU/SC/0138/1958; C.W.S. (India) Limited v. Commissioner of Income Tax MANU/SC/1022/ 1994; Molar Mal (Dead) Through L.Rs. v. M/s. Kay Iron Works(P) Ltd. MANU/SC/0179/2000; Union of India (UOI) and Anr. v. Hansoli Devi and Ors. MANU/SC/0768/2002; Union of India and another v. Pradeep Kumari and others MANU/SC/0450/1995; R.L. Arora v. State of Uttar Pradesh and Ors. MANU/SC/0033/1964; Kedar Nath Singh v. State of Bihar MANU/ SC/0074/1962; Ram Krishna Dalmia v. Shri Justice S.R. Tendolkar and Ors. MANU/SC/0024/1958; In Re: The Special Courts Bill, 1978 MANU/ SC/0039/1978; Shayara Bano and Ors. v. Union of India (UOI) and Ors. MANU/SC/1031/2017; State of U.P. v. Deoman Upadhyaya MANU/SC/ 0060/1960; Lachhman Das on Behalf of Firm Tilak Ram Ram Bux v. State of Punjab and Ors. MANU/SC/0032/1962; Hiral P. Harsora and Ors. v. Kusum Narottamdas Harsora and Ors. MANU/SC/1269/2016; Dr. Subramanian Swamy v. Director, Central Bureau of Investigation and Anr. MANU/SC/ 0417/2014; Secretary Mahatama Gandhi Mission and Ors. v. Bhartiya Kamgar Sena and Ors. MANU/SC/0024/2017; D.S. Nakara and Ors. v. Union of India (UOI) MANU/SC/0237/1982; Anna Bhau Magdum (since deceased by L.R.'s) v. Babasaheb Anandrao Desai MANU/SC/0426/1995; Arjun Hari Kamble v. Anant Mahadev Sawant, 2014 SCC OnLine Bom 4931; Grey v. Pearson (1857) LR 6 HL Cas 61; Warburton v. Loveland (1831) 2 Dow & Clause 480 : 6 ER 806; Salmon v. Duncombe (1886) 11 AC 627; Luke v. Inland Revenue Commissioner (1963) AC 557 : (1964) 54 ITR 692 (HL); Appa Narsappa v. Akubai Ganapati MANU/SC/0375/1999 : (1999) 4 SCC 453

**Case Note:**

Tenancy - Right to purchase - Exercise of - Sections 32,32F,32F(1)(a) and 32G of Maharashtra Tenancy and Agricultural Lands Act, 1948 - Appellants were tenant of property - Bombay Tenancy and Agricultural Lands Act, 1948 was amended by which Section 32 as amended provided that, every tenant shall be deemed to have purchased from landlord free from all encumbrances land held by him as tenant - Proceedings for declaring Appellants as purchaser under Section 32-G of Act were initiated but stand suspended - Appellants came to know that landlady had died and in her place, name of Respondent 1 had been mutated - Appellants filed application before Additional Tahsildar for fixing purchase price under Section 32-G of Act which stand allowed - Respondent 1 filed appeal before Sub-Divisional Officer, who allowed appeal by holding that as no notice having been issued under Section 32F of Act within time, Appellants had lost right of purchase - On further revision against said order, Tribunal confirmed order of Sub-Divisional Officer - Writ petitions were filed by Appellants in High Court, which stand dismissed - Hence, present appeal - Whether object and purpose of amendment made in Section 32-F(1)(a) of Act was applicable for exercise of right to purchase by tenant and successor-in-interest of widow was also obliged to send intimation to tenant of cessation of interest.

**Facts:**

Appellants were tenant of property. The Bombay Tenancy and Agricultural Lands Act, 1948 was amended. Section 32 of Act as amended provided that, every tenant shall be deemed to have purchased from the landlord free from all encumbrances the land held by him as a tenant. The proceedings for declaring the Appellants as purchaser under Section 32-G of Act were initiated during the lifetime of the landlady, the proceedings as contemplated under Section 32-G of Act were suspended. When the Appellants came to know that the landlady had died and in her place, name of Respondent 1 had been mutated, they filed an application before Respondent 2--Additional Tahsildar for fixing the purchase price under Section 32-G of Act. Respondent 2 allowed the application of the Appellants. Aggrieved against the order, Respondent 1 filed an appeal under Section 74 of the 1948 Act before Respondent 3, Sub-Divisional Officer. Respondent 3 allowed the appeal. Respondent 3 held that the Appellant ought to have issued notice under Section 32-F of Act within the time as prescribed and no notice having been issued within the time as prescribed, the Appellants have lost right of purchase. The Appellants, aggrieved by the order of the Sub-Divisional Officer, filed a revision application before the Revenue Tribunal. The Revenue Tribunal confirmed the order of the Sub-Divisional Officer.. Aggrieved against the judgment of the Revenue Tribunal, writ petitions were filed by the Appellants stand dismissed.

**Held, while allowing the appeal:**

(i) Given the fact that the object of the 1956 Amendment, which was an agrarian reform legislation, and was to give the tiller of the soil statutory title to land which such tiller cultivates; and, given the fact that the literal interpretation of Section 32-F(1)(a) of Act would be contrary to justice and reason and would lead to great hardship qua persons who were similarly circumstanced as also to the absurdity of land going back to an absentee landlord when he had lost the right of personal cultivation, in the teeth of the object of the 1956 Amendment, this court delete the words of the fact that he has attained majority. Without these words, therefore, the landlord belonging to all three categories had to send an intimation to the tenant, before the expiry of the period during which such landlord was entitled to terminate the tenancy under Section 31 of Act. [36]

(ii) The Statement of the Objects and Reasons for the 1969 Amendment stated that a large number of cases involving minor landlords had come to the notice of the legislature, for which reason the amnesty scheme mentioned in Sub-section (1A) of Section 32-F of Act was enacted. However, what was forgotten by the draftsman when the addition to Section 32-F(1)(a) of Act was made was the fact that Section 32F(1)(a) of Act referred to three categories of landlords and not only one. The words added by the 1969 amendment thus gave relief to tenants only qua minor landlords and not the other two categories. Obviously, the classification made in favour of tenants of minor landlords as opposed to tenants of landlords of the other two categories is a classification which was arbitrary in nature. This being the case, such classification would ordinarily have to be struck down as being violative of Article 14 of the Constitution of India. [39]

(iii) Instead of striking down such classification as a whole, what could be done was to strike down the words of the fact that he has attained majority, as result of which, what was added by the 1969 Amendment to Section 32-F(1)(a) now ceases to be discriminatory, as it was applicable to tenants of all three categories of landlords. [40]

(iv) The object of the Amendment Act of 1969 was relevant and applicable in deciding the scope of the right to purchase by a tenant of a landlord who was a widow or suffering from mental or physical disability on Tillers' day. The successor-in-interest of a widow was obliged to send an intimation to the tenant of cessation of interest of the widow to enable the tenant to exercise his right of purchase. The decision in Appa Narsappa stands overruled. The decision in Sudam Ganpat stands distinguished. The decision in Tukaram Maruti to the extent that it follows the law laid down in Appa Narsappa, stands overruled. Therefore, set aside the judgment of the High Court. As a result, the tenant's intimation of purchase would now be taken on record by the authorities under the Act, who may now proceed under the Act to determine purchase price and its payment consequent upon which the postponed right of the tenant in this case to own the land would then come into being upon the statutory conditions being met. [50]

**Disposition:** Appeal Allowed

# Independent Thought vs. Union of India (UOI) and Ors. (11.10.2017 - SC) : MANU/SC/ 1298/2017

**Relative Section:**

Child Marriage Restraint Act, 1929 [Repealed] - Section 3, Child Marriage Restraint Act, 1929 [Repealed] - Section 4, Child Marriage Restraint Act, 1929 [Repealed] - Section 5, Child Marriage Restraint Act, 1929 [Repealed] - Section 6; Prohibition of Child Marriage Act 2006 - Section 3, Prohibition of Child Marriage Act 2006 - Section 3(1), Prohibition of Child Marriage Act 2006 - Section 3(2), Prohibition of Child Marriage Act 2006 - Section 9, Prohibition of Child Marriage Act 2006 - Section 10, Prohibition of Child Marriage Act 2006 - Section 11, Prohibition of Child Marriage Act 2006 - Section 13, Prohibition of Child Marriage Act 2006 - Section 14; Protection of Children from Sexual Offences Act, 2012 - Section 2, Protection of Children from Sexual Offences Act, 2012 - Section 3, Protection of Children from Sexual Offences Act, 2012 - Section 4, Protection of Children from Sexual Offences Act, 2012 - Section 5, Protection of Children from Sexual Offences Act, 2012 - Section 6, Protection of Children from Sexual Offences Act, 2012 - Section 7, Protection of Children from Sexual Offences Act, 2012 - Section 8, Protection of Children from Sexual Offences Act, 2012 - Section 9, Protection of Children from Sexual Offences Act, 2012 - Section 10, Protection of Children from Sexual Offences Act, 2012 - Section 11, Protection of Children from Sexual Offences Act, 2012 - Section 12,

Protection of Children from Sexual Offences Act, 2012 - Section 28, Protection of Children from Sexual Offences Act, 2012 - Section 29, Protection of Children from Sexual Offences Act, 2012 - Section 33, Protection of Children from Sexual Offences Act, 2012 - Section 42, Protection of Children from Sexual Offences Act, 2012 - Section 42A; Protection of Human Rights Act, 1993 - Section 2; Protection of Women from Domestic Violence Act, 2005 - Section 3; Juvenile Justice (Care and Protection of Children) Act, 2015 - Section 2(12), Juvenile Justice (Care and Protection of Children) Act, 2015 - Section 2(14), Juvenile Justice (Care and Protection of Children) Act, 2015 - Section 27; Juvenile Justice (Care and Protection of Children) Act, 2000 [Repealed] - Section 2; Medical Termination of Pregnancy Act, 1971; Prohibition of Child Marriage (Karnataka Amendment) Act, 2016 - Section 1(A), Prohibition of Child Marriage (Karnataka Amendment) Act, 2006 - Section 3(1A); Tamil Nadu Buildings (Lease and Rent Control) Act, 1960 - Section 30; Punjab Excise Act, 1914 - Section 30; Industrial Disputes Act, 1947; Life Insurance Corporation Act, 1956; Maharashtra Agricultural Lands (Ceiling on Holdings) Act 1961; Bombay Tenancy and Agricultural Lands (Vidarbha Region) Act, 1958; Dissolution of Muslim Marriages Act, 1939 - Section 2; Hindu Marriage Act, 1955 - Section 13(2); Majority Act, 1875 - Section 2, Majority Act, 1875 - Section 3; Guardians and Wards Act, 1890 - Section 4; Hindu Minority and Guardianship Act, 1956 - Section 4; Representation of the People Act, 1951; Indian Contract Act, 1872 - Section 11; Protection of Children from Sexual Offences Act, 2012; Criminal Law (Amendment) Act, 2013 [Repealed]; Indian Penal Code, 1860 (IPC) - Section 5, Indian Penal Code, 1860 (IPC) - Section 10, Indian Penal Code, 1860 (IPC) - Section 41, Indian Penal Code, 1860 (IPC) - Section 166A, Indian Penal Code, 1860 (IPC) - Section 323, Indian Penal Code, 1860 (IPC) - Section 324, Indian Penal Code, 1860 (IPC) - Section 325, Indian Penal Code, 1860 (IPC) - Section 354, Indian Penal Code, 1860 (IPC) - Section 354A, Indian Penal Code, 1860 (IPC) - Section 354B, Indian Penal Code, 1860 (IPC) - Section 354C, Indian Penal Code, 1860 (IPC) - Section 354D, Indian Penal Code, 1860 (IPC) - Section 370, Indian Penal Code, 1860 (IPC) - Section 370A, Indian Penal Code, 1860 (IPC) - Section 375, Indian Penal Code, 1860 (IPC) - Section 376, Indian Penal Code, 1860 (IPC) - Section 376A, Indian Penal Code, 1860 (IPC) - Section 376C, Indian Penal Code, 1860 (IPC) - Section 376D, Indian Penal Code, 1860 (IPC) - Section 376E, Indian Penal Code, 1860 (IPC) - Section 376(1), Indian Penal Code, 1860 (IPC) - Section

376(2), Indian Penal Code, 1860 (IPC) - Section 497, Indian Penal Code, 1860 (IPC) - Section 509; Constitution of India - Article 9(2), Constitution of India - Article 12, Constitution of India - Article 14, Constitution of India - Article 15, Constitution of India - Article 15(3), Constitution of India - Article 16, Constitution of India - Article 21, Constitution of India - Article 23, Constitution of India - Article 32, Constitution of India - Article 39, Constitution of India - Article 226, Constitution of India - Article 329A(4), Constitution of India - Article 329A(5); Code of Civil Procedure, 1908 (CPC) - Section 56; Code of Criminal Procedure, 1973 (CrPC) - Section 198, Code of Criminal Procedure, 1973 (CrPC) - Section 198(6); Criminal Law (Amendment) Ordinance, 2013

**Hon'bleJudges/Coram:** Madan B. Lokur and Deepak Gupta, JJ.

**Equivalent Citation:** 2017(179)AIC1, AIR2017SC4904, 2018 (1) ALD(Crl.) 128 (SC), 2017 (101) ACC 630, 2017 (3) ALT (Crl.) 379 (A.P.), 2018 1 AWC51SC, 2017(4)BomCR(Cri)599, IV(2017)CCR54(SC), 2018 CriLJ3541, 2017(4)Crimes108(SC), 243(2017)DLT1, III(2017)DMC686SC, 2017/INSC/1030, 2018(1)JLJ401, 2017(4)RCR(Criminal)595, 2017(12)SCALE621, (2017)10SCC800, 2017 (9) SCJ 341, [2017]13SCR821, (2018)1WBLR(SC)19

**NumberofPagesintheOriginalJudgment:** 61

**Case Reference:**

Sri Mahadeb Jiew v. Dr. B.B. Sen MANU/WB/0113/1951 : AIR 1951 Cal 563; Government of A.P. v. P.B. Vijayakumar MANU/SC/0317/1995 : (1995) 4 SCC 520; Yusuf Abdul Aziz v. State of Bombay MANU/SC/0124/1954 : 1954 SCR 930; Cyril Britto v. Union of India MANU/KE/0233/2003 : AIR 2003 Ker 259; Shrikrishna Eknath Godbole v. Union of India PIL No. 166/2016; State of Maharashtra v. Madhukar Narayan Mardikar MANU/SC/0032/1991 : (1991) 1 SCC 57; Suchita Srivastava v. Chandigarh Administration MANU/SC/1580/2009 : (2009) 9 SCC 1; Selvi v. State of Karnataka MANU/SC/0325/2010 : (2010) 7 SCC 263; Ritesh Sinha v. State of Uttar Pradesh MANU/SC/1072/2012 : (2013) 2 SCC 357; Devika Biswas v. Union of India MANU/SC/0999/2016 : (2016) 10 SCC 726; State of Karnataka v. Krishnappa MANU/SC/0210/2000 : (2000) 4 SCC 75; Bodhisattwa Gautam v. Subhra Chakraborty MANU/SC/0245/1996 : (1996) 1 SCC 490; State of Punjab v. Gurmit Singh MANU/SC/0366/1996 : (1996) 2 SCC 384; State of Haryana v. Janak Singh MANU/SC/0570/2013 : (2013) 9 SCC 431; C.R. v. UK; Eisenstadt v. Baird MANU/USSC/0240/1972 : 405 US 438 : 31 L Ed 2d 349 : 92 S Ct 1092; State of Madhya Pradesh

v. Bhopal Sugar Industries Ltd. MANU/SC/0099/1964 : [1964] 6 SCR 846; Rattan Arya v. State of Tamil Nadu MANU/SC/0550/1986 : (1986) 3 SCC 385; Motor General Traders v. State of A.P. MANU/SC/0293/1983 : (1984) 1 SCC 222; Anuj Garg v. Hotel Association of India MANU/SC/8173/2007 : (2008) 3 SCC 1; Satyawati Sharma v. Union of India MANU/SC/1870/2008 : (2008) 5 SCC 287; Life Insurance Corporation of India v. D.J. Bahadur MANU/SC/0305/1980 : (1981) 1 SCC 315; Seaford Court Estates Ltd. v. Asher [1949] 2 K.B. 481 : [1950] A.C. 508; Collector of Customs v. Digvijaya Singhji Spinning & Weaving Mills MANU/SC/0365/1961 : AIR 1961 SC 1549; Jugal Kishore v. State of Maharashtra MANU/SC/0213/1988 : 1989 Supp (1) SCC 589; Abhiram Singh v. C.D. Commachen MANU/SC/0010/2017 : (2017) 2 SCC 629; Association for Social Justice & Research v. Union of India and Ors. MANU/DE/4335/2010 : 2010 (118) DRJ 324 (DB); Court on its own motion (Lajja Devi) and Ors. v. State and Ors. W.P. (Crl.) No. 338 of 2008; T. Sivakumar v. Inspector of Police H.C.P. No. 907 of 2011; Sub-Divisional Magistrate v. Ram Kali MANU/SC/0079/1967 : (1968) 1 SCR 205; Pathumma and Ors. v. State of Kerala and Ors. MANU/SC/0315/1978 : (1978) 2 SCC 1; Government of A.P. v. P. Laxmi Devi MANU/SC/1017/2008 : (2008) 4 SCC 720; Shell Co. of Australia v. Federal Commr. of Taxation 1931 AC 275 : 1930 All ER Rep 671 (PC); Kedar Nath Singh v. State of Bihar MANU/SC/0074/1962 : AIR 1962 SC 955; Subramanian Swamy v. Director, CBI MANU/SC/0417/2014 : (2014) 8 SCC 682; State of Punjab v. Khan Chand MANU/SC/0353/1973 : (1974) 1 SCC 549; Indira Nehru Gandhi v. Raj Narain MANU/SC/0304/1975 : 1975 (Supp.) SCC 1; Keshavananda Bharati v. State of Kerala MANU/SC/0445/1973 : (1973) 4 SCC 225; E.P. Royappa v. State of Tamil Nadu MANU/SC/0380/1973 : (1974) 4 SCC 3; Maneka Gandhi v. Union of India MANU/SC/0133/1978 : (1978) 1 SCC 248; A.L. Kalra v. Project and Equipment Corpn. MANU/SC/0259/1984 : (1984) 3 SCC 316; Babita Prasad v. State of Bihar MANU/SC/0723/1993 : 1993 Supp (3) SCC 268; Ajay Hasia v. Khalid Mujib Sehravardi MANU/SC/0498/1980 : (1981) 1 SCC 722; Dr. K.R. Lakshmanan v. State of Tamil Nadu MANU/SC/0309/1996 : (1996) 2 SCC 226; State of A.P. v. McDowell & Co. MANU/SC/0427/1996 : (1996) 3 SCC 709; Shayara Bano v. Union of India and Ors. (2017) Vol. 8 SCALE 178; Vishakha v. State of Rajasthan MANU/SC/0786/1997 : (1997) 6 SCC 241; Reg v. Clarence (1888) 22 Q.B.D. 23; Rex v. Clarke (1949) 2 All E.R. 448; Justice K.S. Puttaswamy (Retd.) and Anr. v. Union of India and Ors. MANU/SC/1044/2017 : (2017) 10 SCALE 1; Seema (Smt.) v. Ashwani Kumar MANU/SC/

0996/2006 : (2006) 2 SCC 578; Muthamma Devaya and Anr. v. Union of India and Ors. Writ Petition No. 11154/2006 (GM-RES-PIL)

**Case Note:**

Criminal - Child marriage - Validity of consent - Legality of provision - Sections 323, 324, 325, 354 and 375 of Indian Penal Code, 1860, Protection of Children from Sexual Offences Act, 2012, Prohibition of Child Marriage Act, 2006 and Articles 14,15 and 21 of Constitution of India - Petitioner Society had filed petition in public interest with view to draw attention to violation of rights of girls who were married between ages of 15 and 18 years - Hence, present petition - Whether sexual intercourse between a man and his wife being a girl between 15 and 18 years of age was rape - Whether Exception 2 to Section 375 of Code, in so far as it relates to girls aged 15 to 18 years, was unconstitutional and liable to be struck down.

**Facts:**

The Petitioner was a registerd society registered and had since been working in the area of child rights. The society provides technical and hand-holding support to non-governmental organizations as also to government and multilateral bodies in several States in Country. It has also been involved in legal intervention, research and training on issues concerning children and their rights. The society had filed a petition in public interest with a view to draw attention to the violation of the rights of girls who were married between the ages of 15 and 18 years. Hence, present petition.

**Held, while allowing the petition:**

Madan B. Lokur, J.:

(i) Prima facie it might appear that since rape is an offence under the Indian Penal Code (subject to Exception 2 to Section 375) while penetrative sexual assault or aggravated penetrative sexual assault is an offence under the POCSO Act and both are distinct and separate statutes, therefore there is no inconsistency between the provisions of the Indian Penal Code and the provisions of the Protection of Children from Sexual Offences Act, 2012 (POCSO). However the fact was that there was no real distinction between the definition of rape under the Indian Penal Code and the definition of penetrative sexual assault under the POCSO Act. There was also no real distinction between the rape of a married girl child and aggravated penetrative sexual assault punishable under Section 6 of the POCSO Act. Additionally, the punishment for the respective offences was the same, except that the marital rape of a girl child between 15 and 18 years of age was not rape in view of Exception 2 to Section 375 of the Code. In sum, marital rape of a girl child was effectively nothing but aggravated penetrative sexual assault and there was no reason why it should not be punishable under the provisions of the Indian Penal Code. Therefore, it does appear that only a notional or linguistic distinction was sought to be made between rape and penetrative sexual assault and rape of a married girl child and aggravated penetrative sexual assault. There was no rationale for this distinction and it was nothing but a completely arbitrary and discriminatory distinction. [98]

(ii) Exception 2 to Section 375 of the Code to now be meaningfully read as: "Sexual intercourse or sexual acts by a man with his own wife, the wife not being under eighteen years of age, is not rape." It was only through this reading that the intent of social justice to the married girl child and the constitutional vision of the framers of our Constitution could be preserved and protected and perhaps given impetus. [105]

Deepak Gupta, J.:Concurring view

(iii) The State was entitled and empowered to fix the age of consent. The State could make reasonable classification but while making any classification it must show that the classification has been made with the object of achieving a certain end. The classification must have a reasonable nexus with the object sought to be achieved. In this case the justification given by the State was only that it did not want to punish those who consummate their marriage. The stand of the State was that keeping in view the sanctity attached to the institution of marriage, it has decided to make a provision in the nature of Exception 2 to Section 375 od Code. This begs the question as to why in this exception the age has been fixed as 15 years and not 18 years. As pointed out earlier, a girl can legally consent to have sex only after she attains the age of 18 years. She could legally enter into marriage only after attaining the age of 18 years. When a girl gets married below the age of 18 years, the persons who contract such a marriage or abet in contracting such child marriage, commit a criminal offence and were liable for punishment under the Prohibition of Child Marriage Act, 2006. In view of this position there was no rationale for fixing the age at 15 years. This age has no nexus with the object sought to be achieved viz., maintaining the sanctity of marriage because by law such a marriage was not legal. It may be true that this marriage was voidable and not void ab initio (except in the State of Karnataka) but the fact remains that if the girl has got married before the age of 18 years, she has right to get her marriage annulled. Irrespective of the fact that the right of the girl child to get her marriage annulled, it was indisputable that a criminal offence has been committed and other than the girl child, all other persons including her husband, and those persons who were involved in getting her married were guilty of having committed a criminal act. When the State on the one hand, has, by legislation, laid down that abetting child marriage was a criminal offence, it could not, on the other hand defend this classification of girls below 18 years on the ground of sanctity of marriage because such classification has no nexus with the object sought to be achieved. Therefore, also Exception 2 in so far as it relates to girls below 18 years was discriminatory and violative of Article 14 of the Constitution. [183]

(iv) One more ground for holding that Exception 2 to Section 375 of Code was discriminatory was that this was the only provision in various penal laws which gives immunity to the husband. The husband was not immune from prosecution as far as other offences were concerned. Therefore, if the husband beats a girl child and has forcible sexual intercourse with her, he may be charged for offences under Sections 323, 324, 325 of Code etc. but he could not be charged with rape. This leads to an anomalous and astounding situation where the husband could be charged with lesser offences, but not with the more serious offence of rape. As far as sexual crimes against women were concerned, these were covered by Sections 354, 354A, 354B, 354C, 354D of the Code. These relate to assault or use of criminal force against a woman with intent to outrage her modesty; sexual harassment and punishment for sexual harassment; assault or use of criminal force to woman with intent to disrobe; voyeurism; and stalking respectively. There was no exception Clause giving immunity to the husband for such offences. The Domestic Violence Act would also apply in such cases and the husband does not get immunity. There were many other offences where the husband was either specifically liable or may be one of the accused. The husband was not given the immunity in any other penal provision except in Exception 2 to Section 375 of Code. It did not stand to reason that only for the offence of rape the husband should be granted such an immunity especially where the "victim wife" was aged below 18 years i.e. below the legal age of marriage and was also not legally capable of giving consent to have sexual intercourse. Exception 2 to Section 375 of Code was, therefore, discriminatory and violative of Article 14 of the Constitution of India, on this count also. [184]

(v) Exception 2 to Section 375 of Code in so far as it relates to a girl child below 18 years was liable to be struck down on the following grounds:(i) it was arbitrary, capricious, whimsical and violative of the rights of the girl child and not fair, just and reasonable and, therefore, violative of Article 14, 15 and 21 of the Constitution of India; (ii) it was discriminatory and violative of Article 14 of the Constitution of India and; (iii) it was inconsistent with the provisions of POCSO, which must prevail. [195]

# Shyamlal Devda and Ors. vs. Parimala (22.01.2020 – SC) : MANU/SC/0067/2020

**Relative Section:**

Code of Criminal Procedure, 1973 (CrPC) - Section 482; Hindu Marriage Act, 1955 - Section 9; Protection Of Women From Domestic Violence Act, 2005 - Section 18, Protection Of Women From Domestic Violence Act, 2005 - Section 19, Protection Of Women From Domestic Violence Act, 2005 - Section 20, Protection Of Women From Domestic Violence Act, 2005 - Section 27, Protection Of Women From Domestic Violence Act, 2005 - Section 27(1)

**Hon'bleJudges/Coram:** R. Banumathi, A.S. Bopanna and Hrishikesh Roy, JJ.

**Equivalent Citation:** 2020(212)AIC119, AIR2020SC762, 2020(2) AKR 168, 2020 (1) ALD(Crl.) 494 (SC), 2020 (112) ACC 917, 2020(3)BLJ214, 2020(1)CivilCC(S.C.), 2020CriLJ2114, 2020(3)Crimes466(SC), 2020(1)CriminalCC548, I(2020)DMC395SC, 2020(1)HLR414, 2020/INSC/77, 2020(1)JKJ448[SC], 2020(3) KCCR1654, 2020 (1) KHC 876, 2020(1)KLJ799, 2020(1)KLT666, 2020-3-LW413, 2020-1-LW(Crl)799, 2020(1)RCR(Criminal)810, 2020(3)RLW1803(SC), (2020)3SCC14, [2020]1SCR125, 2020(1)UC457

**NumberofPagesintheOriginalJudgment:** 5

**Case Reference: nil**

**Case Note:**

Criminal - Jurisdiction - Quashing of proceedings - Sections 18,19,20,27 and 27(1) of Protection of Women from Domestic Violence Act, 2005 -

Respondent claiming herself to be victim of domestic violence seeking protection order under Section 18 and residence order under Section 19 and monetary relief under Section 20 of Act filed before Court of Metropolitan Magistrate at Bengaluru - Magistrate issued notice to Appellants by holding that Court had jurisdiction to entertain petition filed by Respondent under Section 27 of Act - Aggrieved by issuance of summons, Appellants had filed petition before High Court seeking quashing of entire proceedings - High Court dismissed petition by holding that in complaint filed by Respondent, various instances of domestic violence at different places were narrated by Respondent and therefore, complaint filed in Bengaluru was maintainable - Hence, present appeal - Whether Metropolitan Magistrate court, Bengaluru had jurisdiction to entertain complaint filed by Respondent.

**Facts:**

The Respondent claiming herself to be a victim of domestic violence seeking protection order under Section 18 and residence order under Section 19 and monetary relief under Section 20 of the Act before the Court of Metropolitan Magistrate at Bengaluru against her husband-Appellant No. 14, her in-laws-Appellant Nos. 1 and 2 and other relatives of her husband who are in Chennai, Rajasthan and also in Gujarat. The Magistrate, Bengaluru issued notice to the Appellants by holding that the Court had the jurisdiction to entertain the petition filed by the Respondent under Section 27 of the Domestic Violence Act. Aggrieved by the issuance of summons, the Appellants had filed a petition before the High Court seeking quashing of the entire proceedings. The High Court dismissed the petition by holding that in the complaint filed by the Respondent, various instances of domestic violence at different places were narrated by the Respondent and therefore, the complaint filed in Bengaluru was maintainable under Section 27 of the Domestic Violence Act.

**Held, while partly allowing the appeal:**

(i) The Respondent had made allegations of domestic violence against fourteen Appellants. Appellant No. 14 was the husband and Appellants No. 1 and 2 were the parents-in-law of the Respondent. All other Appellants are relatives of parents-in-law of the Respondent. Appellants No. 3, 5, 9, 11 and 12 were the brothers of father-in-law of the Respondent. Appellants No. 4, 6 and 10 were the wives of Appellants No. 3, 5 and 9 respectively. Appellants No. 7 and 8 were the parents of Appellant No. 1. Appellants No. 1 to 6 and 14 were residents of Chennai. Appellants No. 7 to 10 were the residents of State of Rajasthan and Appellants No. 11 to 13 were the residents of State of Gujarat. Admittedly, the matrimonial house of the Respondent and Appellant No. 1 has been at Chennai. Insofar as Appellant No. 14-husband of the Respondent and Appellants No. 1 and 2-Parents-in-law, there were averments of alleging domestic violence alleging that they had taken away the jewellery of the Respondent gifted to her by her father during marriage and the alleged acts of harassment to the Respondent. There were no specific allegations as to how other relatives of Appellant No. 14 had caused the acts of domestic violence. It was also not known as to how other relatives who were residents of Gujarat and Rajasthan could be held responsible for award of monetary relief to the Respondent. The High Court was not right in saying that there was prima facie case against the other Appellants No. 3 to 13. Since there were no specific allegations against Appellants No. 3 to 13, the criminal case of domestic violence against them could not be continued and was liable to be quashed. [9]

(ii) The Respondent was residing with her parents within the territorial limits of Metropolitan Magistrate Court, Bengaluru. In view of Section 27(1) (a) of the Act, the Metropolitan Magistrate court, Bengaluru had the jurisdiction to entertain the complaint and take cognizance of the offence. There was no merit in the contention raising objection as to the jurisdiction of the Metropolitan Magistrate Court at Bengaluru. [10]

Ratio Decidendi:

The petition under the Domestic Violence Act can be filed in a court where the person aggrieved permanently or temporarily resides or carries on business or is employed.

**Disposition:** Appeal Partly Allowed

# Samir Vidyasagar Bhardwaj vs. Nandita Samir Bhardwaj (09.05.2017 - SC) : MANU/SC/0630/2017

**Relative Section:**

Special Marriage Act - Section 27(1); Protection of Women From Domestic Violence Act, 2005 - Section 19, Protection of Women From Domestic Violence Act, 2005 - Section 19(1); Constitution of India - Article 136

**Hon'bleJudges/Coram:** Kurian Joseph and R. Banumathi, JJ.

**Equivalent Citation:** 2017(4)ABR543, 2017(178)AIC136, AIR2017SC2713, 2017(5)ALD61, 2017 (2) ALD(Crl.) 419 (SC), 2017 (101) ACC 953, 2017 (125) ALR 482, 2017 (4) CCC 398 , 2018(1)CDR12(SC), II (2017) DMC390SC, 2020GLH(2)232, 2017(3)JCC1764, 2017(3)JKJ65[SC], (2017)5MLJ597, 2017 (I) OLR1098, 2017(2)RCR(Civil)1030, 2017(2)RCR(Criminal)968, 2017(4)RLW2747(SC), 2017 (6) SCALE 324, (2017)14SCC583, [2017]4SCR89, 2018 (3) WLN 89 (SC)

**NumberofPagesintheOriginalJudgment: 4**

**Case Reference: nil**

**Case Note:**

Family - Interim order - Removal from own house - Family Court directed Appellant-husband to remove himself from his own home - Not to visit there until divorce petition is finally decided - High Court affirmed interim order passed by Family Court - Hence, present appeal -Whether order directing Appellant-husband to remove himself from matrimonial home of which he was co-owner, was sustainable

**Facts:**

A divorce petition was filed on the ground of cruelty and the Respondent-wife had alleged in the application seeking interim relief that she had been subjected to mental and physical cruelty due to which living under one roof with the Appellant-husband had become impossible. The Family Court passed the interim order directing the Appellant-husband to remove himself out of the matrimonial house and not to visit the same till the decision of the divorce petition. The Appellant-husband approached the High Court stating that final relief sought in the main petition could not have been granted at interim stage; he being a co-owner of the premises, he cannot be evicted from that premises which amounted to his virtual dispossession of the premises of which he was a co-owner. The High Court affirmed the interim order passed by the Family Court. Hence, the present appeal.

**Held, while dismissing the appeal:**

(i) Section 19(1)(b) of the Protection of Women Domestic Violence Act, 2005 provides that the Court may direct the Appellant-husband to remove himself from the shared household. The Family Court arrived at a finding that prima facie material was available on record to accept the allegation of the Respondent-wife on domestic violence wherein the concerned Judge had exercised his discretion Under Section 19(1)(b) which provides that the Magistrate on being satisfied that domestic violence has taken place can remove the spouse from the shared household which in our opinion he has rightly done. Exercise of discretion by Family Court could not be said to be perverse warranting interference. The High Court also considered the factual and legal position. Having gone through the orders of the High Court and the Family Court and considering the fact that the daughters were grown up, the present Court was not inclined to exercise discretions Under Article 136 of the Constitution of India at the interlocutory stage. [11],[12] and[13]

**Disposition:** Appeal Dismissed

# Deoki Panjhiyara vs. Shashi Bhushan Narayan Azad and Ors. (12.12.2012 - SC) : MANU/SC/1096/2012

**Relative Section:**

C ode of Criminal Procedure, 1973 (CrPC) - Section 125; Code of Criminal Procedure, 1973 (CrPC) - Section 198(1)(c); Hindu Marriage Act, 1955 - Section 11, Hindu Marriage Act, 1955 - Section 5; Indian Penal Code 1860, (IPC) - Section 494; Indian Penal Code 1860, (IPC) - Section 495; Protection Of Women From Domestic Violence Act, 2005 - Section 12, Protection Of Women From Domestic Violence Act, 2005 - Section 2, Protection Of Women From Domestic Violence Act, 2005 - Section 2(a), Protection Of Women From Domestic Violence Act, 2005 - Section 2(f), Protection Of Women From Domestic Violence Act, 2005 - Section 2(s); Special Marriage Act, 1954 - Section 13, Special Marriage Act, 1954 - Section 15

**Hon'bleJudges/Coram: P. Sathasivam and Ranjan Gogoi, JJ.**

**Equivalent Citation:** 2013(1)ACR1089, 2013III AD (S.C.) 59, AIR2013SC346, 2013(2)AJR133, 2013(1) AKR 615, 2013(1)ALD(Cri)469, 2013ALLMR(Cri)1099, 2013(3)ALT(Cri)70, 2013(1)ALT(Cri)472, 2013(1) BomCR(Cri)333,I(2013)CCR67(SC),2013CriLJ684,2013(2)CTC232, I(2013)DMC18SC,2013(1)ECrN913,2013 GLH(1)208, 2013(1)HLR207, 2013(1)J.L.J.R.198, 2012(1)JCC502, 2013(1)JCC508, JT2012(12)SC575,

2013-2-LW60,2013-1-LW(Crl)330,2013(1)MLJ(Crl)137, 2013(1)N.C.C.322,2013(I)OLR891,2013(1)PLJR172,2013 (2)RCR(Civil)400, 2013(1)RCR(Criminal)338, 2012(12)SCALE282, (2013)2SCC137, [2012] 11 SCR 825

**NumberofPagesintheOriginalJudgment:** 7

**Case Reference:**

D. Velusamy v. D. Patchaimmal MANU/SC/0872/2010 : (2010) 10 SCC 469; S.P. Changalvaraya Naidu v. Jagannath and Ors. MANU/SC/0192/ 1994 : AIR 1994 SC 853; Yamunabai v. Anantrao AIR 1988 SC 645; M.M. Malhotra v. Union of India MANU/SC/1022/2005 : 2005 (8) SCC 351; A. Subash Babu v. State of Andhra Pradesh and Anr. MANU/SC/0845/2011 : 2011 (7) SCC 616

**Case Note:**

Protection of Women From Domestic Violence Act, 2005 - Sec. 12 - Hindu Marriage Act, 1955 - Sec. 11 - Application for interim maintenance granted by Trial Court and affirmed by Sessions Judge - Writ by husband before High Court - Revision application by husband that the marriage between the appellant and the respondent was null and void - High Court held that the appellant was not the legally wedded wife of the respondent and she was not entitled to maintenance granted by the learned Courts below - Appeal by the appellant-wife - Held, in the present case until the invalidation of the marriage between the appellant and the respondent is made by a competent Court it would only be correct to proceed on the basis that the appellant continues to be the wife of the respondent so as to entitle her to claim all benefits and protection available under the D.V. Act, 2005 -Interference made by the High Court with the grant of maintenance in favour of the appellant was not justified - Order of High Court set aside.

In the present case, if according to the respondent, the marriage between him and the appellant was void on account of the previous marriage between the appellant and Rohit Kumar Mishra the respondent ought to have obtained the necessary declaration from the competent court in view of the highly contentious questions raised by the appellant on the aforesaid score. It is only upon a declaration of nullity or annulment of the marriage between the parties by a competent court that any consideration of the question whether the parties had lived in a "relationship in the nature of marriage" would be justified. In the absence of any valid decree of nullity or the necessarydeclaration the court will have to proceed on the footing that the relationship between the parties is one of marriage and not in the nature of marriage. We would also like to emphasise that any determination of the validity of the marriage between the parties could have been made only by a competent court in an appropriate proceeding by and between the parties and in compliance with all other requirements of law. Mere production of a marriage certificate issued under Section 13 of the Special Marriage Act, 1954 in support of the claimed first marriage of the appellant with Rohit Kumar Mishra was not sufficient for any of the courts, including the High Court, to render a complete and effective decision with regard to the marital status of the parties and that too in a collateral proceeding for maintenance.

**Facts:**

1. The Appellant, who was married to the Respondent in the year 2006, had filed a petition Under Section 12 of the Protection of Women from Domestic Violence Act, 2005 (hereinafter referred to as 'the DV Act') seeking certain reliefs including damages and maintenance. During the pendency of the aforesaid application the Appellant filed an application for interim maintenance which was granted by the learned trial court on 13.02.2008 at the rate of Rs. 2000/- per month. The order of the learned trial court was affirmed by the learned Sessions Judge on 09.07.2008. As against the aforesaid order, the Respondent (husband) filed a Writ Petition before the High Court of Jharkhand.[2]

2. While the Writ Petition was pending, the Respondent sought a recall of the order dated 13.02.2008 on the ground that he could subsequently come to know that his marriage with the Appellant was void on the ground that at the time of the said marriage the Appellant was already married to one Rohit Kumar Mishra. In support, the Respondent - husband had placed before the learned trial court the certificate of marriage dated 18.04.2003 between the Appellant and the said Rohit Kumar Mishra issued by the competent authority Under Section 13 of the Special Marriage Act, 1954 (hereinafter referred to as 'the Act of 1954').[3]

**Held, while allowing the appeal**

1. In the present case, if according to the Respondent, the marriage between him and the Appellant was void on account of the previous marriage between the Appellant and Rohit Kumar Mishra the Respondent ought to have obtained the necessary declaration from the competent court in view of the highly contentious questions raised by the Appellant on the aforesaid score. It is only upon a declaration of nullity or annulment of the marriage between the parties by a competent court that any consideration of the question whether the parties had lived in a "relationship in the nature

of marriage" would be justified. In the absence of any valid decree of nullity or the necessary declaration the court will have to proceed on the footing that the relationship between the parties is one of marriage and not in the nature of marriage. We would also like to emphasise that any determination of the validity of the marriage between the parties could have been made only by a competent court in an appropriate proceeding by and between the parties and in compliance with all other requirements of law. Mere production of a marriage certificate issued Under Section 13 of the Special Marriage Act, 1954 in support of the claimed first marriage of the Appellant with Rohit Kumar Mishra was not sufficient for any of the courts, including the High Court, to render a complete and effective decision with regard to the marital status of the parties and that too in a collateral proceeding for maintenance. Consequently, we hold that in the present case until the invalidation of the marriage between the Appellant and the Respondent is made by a competent court it would only be correct to proceed on the basis that the Appellant continues to be the wife of the Respondent so as to entitle her to claim all benefits and protection available under the DV Act, 2005.[19]

2. Our above conclusion would render consideration of any of the other issues raised wholly unnecessary and academic. Such an exercise must surely be avoided.[20]

3. We, accordingly, hold that the interference made by the High Court with the grant of maintenance in favour of the Appellant was not at all justified. Accordingly, the order dated 09.04.2010 passed by the High Court is set aside and the present appeals, are allowed.[21]

# Saraswathy vs. Babu (25.11.2013 - SC) : MANU/SC/ 1193/2013

**Relative Section:**

Code of Criminal Procedure, 1973 (CrPC) - Section 125; Hindu Marriage Act, 1955 - Section 13(1)(ia), Hindu Marriage Act, 1955 - Section 9; Protection Of Women From Domestic Violence Act, 2005 - Section 12, Protection Of Women From Domestic Violence Act, 2005 - Section 18, Protection Of Women From Domestic Violence Act, 2005 - Section 19, Protection Of Women From Domestic Violence Act, 2005 - Section 2(g), Protection Of Women From Domestic Violence Act, 2005 - Section 20, Protection Of Women From Domestic Violence Act, 2005 - Section 20(d), Protection Of Women From Domestic Violence Act, 2005 - Section 22, Protection Of Women From Domestic Violence Act, 2005 - Section 3, Protection Of Women From Domestic Violence Act, 2005 - Section 3(iv), Protection Of Women From Domestic Violence Act, 2005 - Section 31, Protection Of Women From Domestic Violence Act, 2005 - Section 32

**Hon'bleJudges/Coram:** S.J. Mukhopadhaya and V. Gopala Gowda, JJ.

**Equivalent Citation:** 2014(1)ACR495, 2013XII AD (S.C.) 54, 2014(133)AIC20, AIR2014SC857, 2014(2)AJR554, 2014 (1) ALD(Crl.) 1032 (SC), 2014 (84) ACC 394, 2013ALLMR(Cri)4486, 2013 ALL MR (Cri)4486(SC), 2014 (1) ALT (Crl.) 522 (A.P.), 2014(1)BomCR(Cri)356, 2014 (2) CCC 73 , I(2014) CCR3 (SC), 2014CriLJ1000, 2013(4)Crimes610(SC), 2014(I)CLR(SC)78, I(2014)DMC3, I(2014)DMC03, 2014 (1) ECrN 1145, 2014(1)HLR81, 2014(1)J.L.J.R.578, JT2013(15)SC129, 2013 (4) KHC 735, 2014-1-LW294, 2014-1-LW(Crl)62,

2013(4)MLJ(Crl)746, 2014(1)N.C.C.146, 2014(I)OLR(SC)432, 2014(2)PLJR30, (2014) 175 PLR759, 2014(1)RCR(Criminal)167, 2013(14)SCALE370, (2014)3SCC712, 2014 (2) SCJ 745, [2013] 12 SCR 914, 2014(1)UC158

**NumberofPagesintheOriginalJudgment:** 9

**Case Reference:** V.D. Bhanot v. Savita Bhanot MANU/SC/0115/2012 : (2012) 3 SCC 183

**Case Note:**

Protection of Women from Domestic Violence Act, 2005 - Section 18 and 19--Protection/residence, maintenance--Granting of--Held--In spite of order of court, if there is noncompliance of order, husband is entitle to give protection/residence/maintenance to the wife--Hence directed husband to pay 5 lacs rupees to appellant as compensation for harassment--Direction issued.

Protection of Women from Domestic Violence Act, 2005 - Section 18 and 19--Prior conduct of parties--Scope--Held--Before passing an order under Section 18 and 19 of Act 2005, it is just for court to consider the conduct of parties prior passing the order.

**Facts:**

1. The pertinent facts of the case are as follows:

The parties to the present dispute are married to each other and the said marriage was solemnized on 17th February, 2000. According to the Appellant, she brought 50 sovereign gold ornaments and 1 kg silver articles as stridhan also Rs. 10,000/- was given to the Respondent. After marriage the Appellant lived in her matrimonial house at Padi, Chennai. After four months of the marriage, the Respondent-husband and his family demanded more dowry in the form of cash and jewels. The Appellant was not able to satisfy the said demand. Therefore, she was thrown out of her matrimonial house by the Respondent and her in-laws. Another allegation of the Appellant is that after sending out the Appellant from her matrimonial house, the Respondent-husband intended to marry again. On hearing such rumour, the Appellant filed petition Under Section 9 of the Hindu Marriage Act, 1955 (hereinafter referred to as, "the HM Act, 1955") bearing No. H.M.O.P. No. 216 of 2001 before the Principal Subordinate Judge, Chengalpattu, Tamil Nadu for restitution of conjugal rights.

The Respondent-husband on the other hand filed H.M.O.P. No. 123 of 2002 Under Section 13(1)(ia) and (iv) of the HMA Act, 1955 before the Principal Subordinate Judge, Chengalpattu, Tamil Nadu for dissolution of marriage between the Appellant and the Respondent.

On 5th April, 2006, the learned Principal Subordinate Judge, Chengalpattu, Tamil Nadu dismissed the petition for dissolution of marriage filed by the Respondent-husband and allowed the petition for restitution of conjugal rights filed by the Appellant-wife with the condition that the Appellant should not insist for setting up of a separate residence by leaving the matrimonial home of the Respondent.

In the year 2008, the Appellant filed Crl. M.P. No. 2421 of 2008 before learned XIII Metropolitan Magistrate, Egmore, Chennai against the Respondent seeking relief Under Section 19, 20 and 22 of the Protection of Women from Domestic Violence Act, 2005 (hereinafter referred to as, "the PWD Act, 2005"). The learned XIII Metropolitan Magistrate, Egmore, Chennai partly allowed the same and directed the Respondent to give maintenance of Rs. 2,000/- per month to the Appellant to meet out her medical expenses, food, shelter and clothing expenses. The Magistrate Court's held that the Appellant is in domestic relationship with the Respondent and the Appellant being the wife of the Respondent has a right to reside in the shared household. The officer in charge of the nearest Police Station was directed to give protection to the Appellant for implementation of the residence orders and was also directed to assist in the implementation of the protection order.

The Respondent-husband being aggrieved preferred Criminal Appeal No. 339 of 2008 before the Sessions Court (Vth Additional Judge) at Chennai.

In the meantime, as per the order passed by the XIII Metropolitan Magistrate, Egmore, Chennai the Appellant-wife went to her matrimonial house for staying with the Respondent-husband house along with Protection Officer. However, the Respondent did not obey the order of the Court and refused to allow the Appellant-wife to enter the house and locked the door from outside and went out.

On 22nd December, 2008, the Appellant filed a complaint against the Respondent for not obeying the order of the learned XIII Metropolitan Magistrate, Egmore, Chennai and the same was registered in Ambatur T3 Korattur Police Station as FIR No. 947 of 2008 Under Section 31, 32 and 74 of the PWD Act, 2005. The case was committed to the learned XIII Metropolitan Magistrate, Egmore, Chennai and registered as Criminal Miscellaneous Petition No. 636 of 2011.

In the meantime, the Criminal Appeal No. 339 of 2008 filed by the Respondent-husband was partly allowed by the Sessions Court (Vth Addl. Judge) at Chennai on 21st October, 2010. Sessions Courts by the said order set aside the order prohibiting the Respondent-husband from committing acts of domestic violence as against the Appellant-wife by not allowing her to live in the shared household and the order directing the Respondent to reside in the house owned by Respondent's mother and upheld the order granting maintenance of Rs. 2,000/- per month in favour of the Appellant-wife by the Respondent-husband.

**Held, while allowing the appeal**

1. We are of the view that the act of the Respondent-husband squarely comes within the ambit of Section 3 of the PWD Act, 2005, which defines "domestic violence" in wide term. The High Court made an apparent error in holding that the conduct of the parties prior to the coming into force PWD Act, 2005 cannot be taken into consideration while passing an order. This is a case where the Respondent-husband has not complied with the order and direction passed by the Trial Court and the Appellate Court.[15]

He also misleads the Court by giving wrong statement before the High Court in the contempt petition filed by the Appellant-wife. The Appellant-wife having being harassed since 2000 is entitled for protection orders and residence orders Under Section 18 and 19 of the PWD, Act, 2005 along with the maintenance as allowed by the Trial Court Under Section 20(d) of the PWD, Act, 2005. Apart from these reliefs, she is also entitled for compensation and damages for the injuries, including mental torture and emotional distress, caused by the acts of domestic violence committed by the Respondent-husband. Therefore, in addition to the reliefs granted by the courts below, we are of the view that the Appellant-wife should be compensated by the Respondent-husband. Hence, the Respondent is hereby directed to pay compensation and damages to the extent of Rs. 5,00,000/- in favour of the Appellant-wife.

16. The order passed by the High Court is set aside with a direction to the Respondent-husband to comply with the orders and directions passed by the courts below with regard to residence and maintenance within three months. The Respondent-husband is further directed to pay a sum of Rs. 5,00,000/- in favour of the Appellant-wife within six months from the date of this order. The appeal is allowed with aforesaid observations and directions. However, there shall be no separate order as to costs.[16]

# Adv. Jayprakash Somani's Videos On Law

**Adv. Jayprakash Somani's Videos on Law on Youtube- 'jaysomani64' channel.**

1) SLP in Supreme Court / Special Leave Petitions in the Supreme Court of India

2) Transfer of Civil & Criminal Cases by the Supreme Court of India / Transfer of Matrimonial Cases

3) Appellate Jurisdiction of the Supreme Court of India

4) Jurisdictions of the Supreme Court of India

5) Public Interest Litigation in the Supreme Court of India / PIL in Supreme Court

6) Article 32 Writ Petitions in the Supreme Court of India

7) Bail Matters Top 10 Supreme Court Cases

8) FIR Quashing in High Court & Supreme Court

9) Bail & Anticipatory Bail Matters in Supreme Court

10) Insolvency & Bankruptcy Matters in the Supreme Court

11) Insolvency & Bankruptcy Code 2016 Part 1

12) Insolvency & Bankruptcy Code 2016 Part 2

13) Insolvency & Bankruptcy Code 2016 Part 3

14) Corporate Liquidation Process

15) Supreme Court Rules & Procedures Webinar of 2.5 hour on Zoom

16) RDDBFI Act, 1993 (Introduction)

17) The Indian Contact Act 1872

18) Negotiable Instruments Act (Introduction)

19) How to avoid matrimonial disputes& some more videos

20) SEBI Matters in the Supreme Court

21) Matrimonial Matters: Supreme Court's 20 Case Laws

22) Consumer Matters Supreme Court's 20 Case Laws

23) Service Matters Supreme Court's 20 Case Laws

24) How to Search Lawyer for Your Matter

25) Property Matters Supreme Court's 20 Case Laws

26) Bail Matters: Supreme Court's 20 Case Laws

27) Supreme Court / High Court Vacation Benches

28) 69000 Teacher's Recruitment Matters of UP Government in the Supreme Court

29) Contempt of Court Matters in the Supreme Court

30) Advocate Act's Matters in the Supreme Court

31) Business Law Matters in the Supreme Court

32) Banking Matters in the Supreme Court

33) Labour Law Matters in the Supreme Court

34) Arbitration Matters in the Supreme Court

35) Careers in Law -Zoom Webinar by Adv. Jayprakash Somani

36) Civil Matters in the Supreme Court

37) Consumer Protection Act | Consumer Matters in the Supreme Court

38) Corporate Matters in the Supreme Court

39) Criminal Matters in the Supreme Court

40) Role of Respondent in the Supreme Court of India

41) Motor Vehicle Accident Matters in Supreme Court with case laws

42) Article 131 Original Suits in Supreme Court

43) PIL in Supreme Court/ Public Interest Litigations in the Supreme Court of India'

44) CAB Citizenship Amendment Bill is not Unconstitutional

45) Supreme Court of India Cases & Process – Marathi

46) Legal Services Export / Export of Legal Services

47) Transfer of Matrimonial Cases by the Supreme Court of India

48) Public Interest Litigation PIL

49) The Specific Relief Act (Introduction)

50) Corporate Insolvency Resolution Process CIRP

51) ABMM's Career 5 - Careers in Law

52) Transfer of cases by Supreme Court

53) Writ Petitions in High Court & Supreme Court of India

54) Supreme Court Jurisdictions - Appeals, SLP, Writ Petitions, Transfer, Original, Review, Curative

55) LEGAL INDIA TV Show: Cases Handled in Supreme Court

56) Corporate Liquidation Process

57) Legal Services Export / Export of Legal Services

58) Corporate Laws

59) Election Matters- Supreme Court's 20 Case Laws

60) Companies Act, 2013

62) Competition Act, 2002

63) Banking Matters - Supreme Court's 20 Case Laws

64) Election Matters in the Supreme Court

65) Armed Forces Tribunal Matters in the Supreme Court

66) Compassionate Appointment Service matter

**67)** Foreign Exchange Management Act FEMA

**68)** Foreign Trade Policy 2021-26 Proposed

**69)** Customs Act 1962

**70)** Narcotic Drugs and Psychotropic Substances Act, 1985 NDPS Act

**71)** Foreign Trade Development & Regulation Act, 1992

**72)** How to Search Good Advocate in the Supreme Court of India

**73)** Sr. Adv Vikas Singh's Interview in Nani Palkhivala Wednesday Law Club

**74)** Indian Penal Code (I. P. C.)

**75)** Criminal Procedure Code (Cr. P. C.)

**76)** Commercial Courts & International Arbitration - by Mr. Jaideep Gupta, Senior Advocate in Nani Palkhivala Wednesday Law Club

**77)** Sr. Adv Ranji Thomos in Nani Palkhivala Wednesday Law Club

**78)** Urgent Matters in Supreme Court during vacations

**79)** 498A Bail Matters in Supreme Court

**81)** 376 Bail Matters in Supreme Court

**82)** 302, 304, 307, 308 Bail Matters in Supreme Court

**83)** 138, 420 Bail Matters in Supreme Court

**84)** POCSO Act Bail Matters in Supreme Court

**85)** NDPS Act Bail Matters in Supreme Court

**86)** What is ED (Enforcement Directorate)?

**87)** Prevention of Money Laundering Act, 2002 (PMLA Act)

**88)** Insolvency & Bankruptcy Code- Supreme Court Case Laws. Webinar in Nani Palkhivala Wednesday Law Club

**89)** What is NCLT & NCLAT?

**90)** Acquittal from 376- Supreme Court's some case laws in Nani Palkhivala Wednesday Law Club dt 28.7.22

**91)** Insolvency & Bankruptcy in India

**92)** Can we file case directly in the Supreme Court?

**93)** Adv. Anuja Pethia has cleared AOR Exam 2021 with 77% marks - Her interview in Nani Palkhivala Wednesday Law Club

**94)** Customs Act - Supreme Court Case Laws & Interview of AOR Adv. Anuja Pethia in Nani Palkhivala Law Club.

**95)** The Uttar Pradesh Public Service Tribunals Act, 1976

**96)** POCSO Act - Supreme Court Case Laws & Interview of AOR Adv. Shoumendu Mukharji & Adv. Nishant Verma in Nani Palkhivala Law Club.

**97)** Who Can Trigger CIRP Process Under Insolvency Law of India

**98)** The Uttar Pradesh Government Servant Discipline and Appeal Rules, 1999

**99)** CIRP Application Under Sec 7 by FC

**100)** Information Technology Act 2000

**101)** Uttar Pradesh Recruitment of Dependants of Government Servants Dying in Harness Rules, 1974

**102)** Foreign Exchange Management Act 1999 & Supreme Court's Case Laws on FEMA & Leading Case of AOR Exam in Nani Palkhivala Law Club.

**103)** Arbitration and Conciliation Act 1996 & It's Supreme Court Case Laws in Nani Palkhivala Wednesday Law Club.

**104)** Narcotic Drugs & Psychotropic Substances Act 1985 (NDPS Act) & It's Supreme Court Case Laws in Nani Palkhivala Wednesday Law Club.

**105)** Recovery of Debts and Bankruptcy Act 1993

**106)** Uttar Pradesh Land Revenue Code 2006

**107)** CIRP Application Under Sec 9 by OC

**108)** CIRP Application Under Sec 10 by CD

**109)** Hindu Succession Act, 1956

**110)** Maharashtra Civil Services Rules, 1981

**111)** Indian Contract Act, 1872 & Supreme Court's Case Laws" in Nani Palkhiwala Wednesday Law Club

**112)** Securities and Exchange Board of India Act, 1992 i. e. SEBI Act 1992 & Case Laws on Insiders Trading" in Nani Palkhiwala Wednesday Law Club

**113)** Moratorium Under Section 14 of IBC, 2016

**114)** Hindu Marriage Act, 1955

**115)** Maharashtra Land Revenue Code, 1966

**116)** 64 Leading Cases of AOR Exam Session 1 :- Cases 1 to16 in Nani Palkhiwala Wednesday Law Club

**117)** 64 Leading Cases of AOR Exam Session 2: Cases 17 to 32 in Nani Palkhiwala Wednesday Law Club

**118)** 64 Leading Cases of AOR Examination Session 3: Cases 33 to 48 in Nani Palkhivala Wednesday Law Club

**119)** 64 Leading Cases of AOR Exam Session 4: Cases 49 to 64 in Nani Palkhivala Wednesday Law Club

**120)** Labour Laws of India: Part 1 - 4 New Labour Law Codes of India

**121)** New Labour Laws Part 2 The Code on Wages, 2019

**122)** New Labour Laws Part 3:- The Code on Social Security, 2020

**123)** Argue in English Fluently & Confidently - Two months online course.

**124)** SLP Admission in the Supreme Court. 2023 ( Hindi)

**125)** Transfer of Petitions from the Supreme Court ( Hindi )

**126)** Review Petition in the Supreme Court.( Hindi )

**127)** Recovery of debts from the Company ( Hindi )

**128)** How to search 'Good Insolvency & Bankruptcy Consultant?' (HINDI)

**129)** Curative Petition in the Supreme Court

**130)** AFT Appeals in the Supreme Court ( HINDI )

**131)** NCLAT's Appeals in the Supreme Court.

**132)** Transfer Petition: Which matters can we transfer?

**133)** SLP Types of SLP in the Supreme court of India ( English ).

**134)** Argue in English Fluently and Confidently in the High Court & Supreme Court'.

# List Of Adv. Jayprakash Somani's Published Books

1. Supreme Court of India's Leading Case Laws on 'Insolvency & Bankruptcy Code 2016'

2. Bail Matters – Supreme Court's Latest Leading Case Laws

3. Arbitration Matters- Supreme Court's Latest Leading Case Laws

4. Property Matters - Supreme Court's Latest Leading Case Laws

5. Matrimonial Matters- Supreme Court's Latest Leading Case Laws

6. Election Matters- Supreme Court's Latest Leading Case Laws

7. SEBI Matters- Supreme Court's Latest Leading Case Laws

8. Banking Matters- Supreme Court's Latest Leading Case Laws

9. Service Matters- Supreme Court's Latest Leading Case Laws

10. Contempt of Court Matters- Supreme Court's Latest Leading Case Laws

11. Consumer Protection Matters- Supreme Court's Latest Leading Case Laws

12. Corporate Law- Supreme Court's Latest Leading Case Laws

13. Supreme Court's AOR Exam- Leading Cases

14. Armed Force Tribunal - Supreme Court's Latest Leading Case Laws

15. Acquittal From 376 - Supreme Court's Latest Leading Case Laws

16. Negotiable instrument – Supreme Court's Latest Leading Case Laws

17. Contract Act- Supreme Court's Latest Leading Case Laws

18. Insider trading- Supreme Court's Latest Leading Case Laws

19. Foreign Exchange and Management Act- Supreme Court's Latest Leading Case Laws

20. Income Tax Act- Supreme Court's Latest Leading Case Laws

21. Company Law- Supreme Court's Latest Leading Case Laws

22. Competition & Monopoly Matters- Supreme Court's Latest Leading Case Laws

23. Compassionate Appointment- Service Matters- Supreme Court's Latest Leading Case Laws

24. Compulsory Retirement- Service Matters- Supreme Court's Latest Leading Case Laws

25. Voluntary Retirement- Service Matters- Supreme Court's Latest Leading Case Laws

26. Removal/Dismissal/Termination from Service- Supreme Court's Latest Leading Case Laws

27. Seniority- Service Matter- Supreme Court's Latest Leading Case Laws

28. Promotion- Service Matter- Supreme Court's Latest Leading Case Laws

29. Equal Pay for Equal Work- Service Matter- Supreme Court's Latest Leading Case Laws

30. Condition of Service- Service Matter- Supreme Court's Latest Leading Case Laws

31. Customs Act- Supreme Court's Leading Case Laws

32. Information Technology Act- Supreme Court's Leading Case Laws

33. SEC. 125 CR. P. C.- Supreme Court's Leading Case Laws

34. SEC. 498A OF I. P. C.- Supreme Court's Leading Case Laws

35. MOTOR VEHICLE ACT- Supreme Court's Leading Case Laws

36. CONDITION OF SERVICE- SERVICE MATTER- Supreme Court's Leading Case Laws

37. SUSPENSION- SERVICE MATTER- Supreme Court's Leading Case Laws

38. Reservation in SC, ST, OBC- Service Matter- Supreme Court's Leading Case Laws

39. NARCOTIC DRUGS AND PSYCHOTROPIC SUBSTANCES (NDPS) ACT - Supreme Court of India's Latest Leading Case Laws

40. SEC 302 IPC - Supreme Court of India's Latest Leading Case Laws

41. PROTECTION OF CHILDREN FROM SEXUAL OFFENCES ACT (POCSO) - Supreme Court of India's Latest Leading Case Laws

42. PMLA ACT BAIL MATTERS - Supreme Court of India's Leading Case Laws

43. SEC 376 BAIL MATTERS - Supreme Court of India's Leading Case Laws

44. SEC 302 BAIL MATTERS - Supreme Court of India's Leading Case Laws

45. POCSO ACT BAIL MATTERS - Supreme Court of India's Leading Case Laws

46. JUVENILE JUSTICE ACT- Supreme Court of India's Leading Case Laws

47. TRANSFER OF PROPERTY ACT- Supreme Court of India's Leading Case Laws

48. PROFESSIONAL ETHICS OF ADVOCATES- AOR EXAM- SUPREME COURT'S LEADING CASE LAWS

**49.** WHITE COLLAR CRIME- SUPREME COURT'S LEADING CASE LAWS

**50.** SEC 302 BAIL MATTERS- SUPREME COURT'S LEADING CASE LAWS

**51.** SEC 7 IBC 2016 - SUPREME COURT'S LATEST LEADING CASE LAW

**52.** ADVERSE POSSESSION IN PROPERTY MATTER - SUPREME COURT'S LATEST LEADING CASE LAWS

**53.** ARMED FORCE TRIBUNAL ACT- SUPREME COURT'S LATEST LEADING CASE LAWs

**54.** ESSENTIAL COMMODITIES ACT 1955- SUPREME COURT'S LATEST LEADING CASE LAWS

**55.** 'FOOD SAFETY AND STANDARD ACT 2006' - SUPREME COURT AND HIGH COURT's LEADING CASE LAWS

**56.** 'FOREIGN TRADE DEVELOPMENT AND REGULATION ACT'- SUPREME COURT AND HIGH COURT'S LEADING CASE LAWS

**57.** 'PARTNERSHIP ACT 1932'- SUPREME COURT'S LEADING CASE LAWS

**58.** 'COTPA ACT 2003' - SUPREME COURT AND HIGH COURT'S LEADING CASE LAWS

**Books are available online in India**

**1.** Notion Press: https://notionpress.com/author/jayprakash_somani

**2.** Amazon: https://www.amazon.in/s?k=jayprakash+somani

**3.** Flipkart: https://www.flipkart.com/search?q=Jayprakash%20Somani

**Books are available online at International Market**

**4.** Amazon International: https://www.amazon.com/s?k=jayprakash+somani

**5.** Amazon United Kingdom: https://www.amazon.co.uk/s?k=jayprakash+somani

**6.** E-Books/Kindle edition at National & International Level: https://www.amazon.in/s?k=jaypraksh+somani

# Adv Jayprakash Somani's Online Courses

**Download our app** to get access to our Free Videos, Free Bare Acts, Free Study Material in Legal as well as International Business Regime.

**Android App Link** ;-https://clpandrea.page.link/cmSm

**Ios APp Link** :-https://apps.apple.com/us/app/classplus/id1324522260

**Login with org code** ;- (qywzji)

**Web Link** ;-https://qywzji.courses.store/

Download App on Google play store - Type

**<u>Jayprakash Somani SupremeCourt</u>**

**Legal Courses :**

**1. SLP- Bail Matters- Drafting & Successful Arguing in the Supreme Court.**

**Description** - This Course is helpful to Advocates, Litigants, Law Officers, Law Students, Law Schools, Individual. Course contains 8 Videos + Study Material+ PDF Books. Access to this course is for Two Years. Expected duration of this course is one month only.

**Topics :** 1. SLP- Bail Matters- Drafting & Successful Arguing in the Supreme Court, **2.** Types of bails, **3.** Laws related to bail matters, **4.** How to read Impugned Order of High Court & frame substantial question of laws, **5.** How to draft excellent SLP, **6.** Searching of citations/ case laws, **7.** How to argue in admission hearings, **8.** How argue in after notice hearing.

**Speaker:** Jayprakash Bansilal Somani, MBA (Foreign Trade), LL. B. Advocate, Supreme Court of India & IP www.jayprakashsomani.com Call: P. A. 9322188701

**2. SLP- Succession Matters- Drafting & Successful Arguing in the Supreme Court.**

**Description** - This Course is helpful to Advocates, Litigants, Law Officers, Law Students, Law Schools, Individual. Course contains 9 Videos + Study Material+ PDF Books. Access to this course is for Two Years. Expected duration of this course is one month only.

**Topics :1.** SLP- Succession Matters- Drafting & Successful Arguing in the Supreme Court, **2.** Information about Succession Matters, **3.** Laws related to Succession Matters, **4.** How to read Impugned Order of High Court to frame substantial questions of law, **5.** How to draft excellent synopsis & list of date, **6.** Drafting of SLP of Succession Matter, **7.** Searching of citations/ case laws, **8.** How to prepare notes & then argue in admission hearings, **9.** How to prepare notes & then argue in after notice final hearing.

**Speaker:** Jayprakash Bansilal Somani, MBA (Foreign Trade), LL. B. Advocate, Supreme Court of India & IP www.jayprakashsomani.com Call: P. A. 9322188701

**3. Legal Vocabulary & its practice pattern to Argue in High Court and Supreme Court / Improve Your Legal English**

**Description** - This Course is helpful to Advocates, Litigants, Law Officers, Law Students, Law Schools, Individual. Course contains 11 Videos + Study Material+ PDF Books. Access to this course is for Two Years. Expected duration of this course is three month only.

**Topics :** **1.** Legal Vocabulary & its practice pattern to Argue in High Court and Supreme Court / Improve Your Legal English, **2.** 1000 legal verbs with its three forms, **3.** Twelve Tenses with its running practice, **4.** One Pdf book on legal vocabulary & its practice pattern with Latin Terms, **5.** Second Pdf book on legal vocabulary & its practice pattern with Latin Terms, **6.** Some Videos of CJI Dr. Dhananjay Chandrachud for the practice of good legal English, **7.** Some Video/Audio Lectures of Legend Nani Palkhivala for standard perfect legal English & flow of Speech, **8.** Some Videos of renowned Sr. Advocates from Mumbai for flow, legal vocabulary & their struggle in legal journey, **9.** Some Videos of Sr. Advocates of the Supreme Court for flow & legal vocabulary, **10.** Some Videos of foreign persons to improve Professional English & thinking process in English, **11.**

Some important legal doctrines with case laws.

**Speaker:** Jayprakash Bansilal Somani, MBA (Foreign Trade), LL. B. Advocate, Supreme Court of India & IP www.jayprakashsomani.com Call: P. A. 9322188701.

**4. SLP- Property Matters - Drafting and Successful Arguing in the Supreme Court.**

**Description** - This Course is helpful to Advocates, Litigants, Law Officers, Law Students, Law Schools 8 Individual. Course contains 9 Videos + Study Material+ PDF Books. Access to this course is for Two Years. Expected duration of this course is one month only.

**Topics :** 1. SLP- Property Matters - Drafting and Successful Arguing in the Supreme Court, **2.** Types of Property Matters, **3.** Laws related to Property Matters, **4.** How to read Impugned Order of High Court to guide client & frame substantial question of laws, **5.** How to draft Synopsis & List of Dates in Property Matter, **6.** How to draft excellent SLP of Property Matter, **7.** Searching of citations/ case laws with specific paras, **8.** How to argue confidently in admission hearings, **9.** How argue confidently in after notice & final hearings.

**Speaker:** Jayprakash Bansilal Somani, MBA (Foreign Trade), LL. B. Advocate, Supreme Court of India & IP www.jayprakashsomani.com Call: P. A. 9322188701.

**International Business Courses -**

**1. Agri Products Exports - Scope from India.**

**Description** - This Course is helpful to Agriculturalists, Entrepreneurs, Exporters, Importers, Students. Course contains 12 Videos + Study Material+ PDF Books. Access to this course is for Two Years. Expected duration of this course is one month only.

**Topics :** **1**- Agri Products Exports - Scope from India, **2.** Agri Export's share in India's total export, **3.** Agri Export Promotional Council's Support, **4.** Top 10 Agri export countries, **5.** Top 10 Agri export product, **6.** India's share in World's Agri Exports, **7.** Onion Exports from India, **8.** Rice Exports from India, **9.** Mango Exports from India, **10.** Fresh Vegetable Exports, **11.** Fresh Fruits Exports, **12.** Export of Agri Allied Products.

**Speaker:** Jayprakash Bansilal Somani, MBA (Foreign Trade), LL. B. Advocate, Supreme Court of India & IP www.jayprakashsomani.com Call: P. A. 9322188701.

**2. Textile Exports - Scope from India.**

**Description** - This Course is helpful to Textile Business Houses, Entrepreneurs, Exporters, Importers, Students. Course contains 14 Videos + Study Material+ PDF Books. Access to this course is for Two Years. Expected duration of this course is one month only.

**Topics : 1**- Textile Exports - Scope from India, **2.** Textile Export's share in India's total exports, **3.** Support of Textile Export Promotional Council, **4.** Top 10 Countries in Textile Exports, **5.** Top 10 Products in Textile Exports, **6.** Export of Readymade Garments, **7.** Export of Man-made Textiles, **8.** Export of Handloom Products, **9.** Export of Wool & Woollen Textiles, **10.** Export of Silk, **11.** Exports of Handicrafts & Carpets, **12.** Exports of Coir & Coir Manufacturers, **13.** Exports of Jute,14. India's share in World's total textile expor.

**Speaker:** Jayprakash Bansilal Somani, MBA (Foreign Trade), LL. B. Advocate, Supreme Court of India & IP www.jayprakashsomani.com Call: P. A. 9322188701.

**3. Export Import Procedure -Perfect Documentation & It's Management.**

**Description** -This Course is helpful to Business Men, Service Providers, Entrepreneurs, Exporters, Importers, Students. Course contains 13 Videos + Study Material+ PDF Books. Access to this course is for Two Years. Expected duration of this course is three months only.

**Topics : 1.** Export Import Procedure, Perfect Documentation & Its management, **2.** Company Formation, **3.** Opening of Bank Account in AD Bank, **4.** Export Procedure points, **5.** Import Procedure Points, **6.** Taking Import Export Code, **7.** Taking RCMC number, **8.** Registration at Port when necessary, **9.** Quality Inspection Certificate of Goods, **10.** CHA & its roll, **11.** Custom Formalities, **12.** Export Documents such as Invoice, Bill of Lading, Insurance Certificate, Quality Inspection Certificate & others, **13.** Excellent Management of Export & Imports Documents.

**Speaker:** Jayprakash Bansilal Somani, MBA (Foreign Trade), LL. B. Advocate, Supreme Court of India & IP www.jayprakashsomani.com Call: P. A. 9322188701.

**4. Jewellery Exports -Scope from India**

**Description** - You can understand world wide scope for Jems & Jewellery in multidimensional ways. 14 videos of this course will create positive spark among you to enter into the Exports & Imports of Gems & Jewellery and other products. Chance to ask your query to Somani Sir every week.

**Topics :1.** Jewellery Exports - Scope from India, **2.** Jewellery Export's share in India's total exports, **3.** Support of Jems & Jewellery Export Promotional Council, **4.** Top 10 Countries in Jewellery Exports, **5.** Top 10 Products in Jewellery Exports, **6.** Export of Cut & Polished Diamonds, **7.** Export of Gold Jewellery, **8.** Export of Plain Gold Jewellery, **9.** Export of Studded Gold Jewellery, **10.** Export of Silver Jewellery, **11.** Exports of Platinum Jewellery, **12.** Exports of Imitation Jewellery, **13.** Exports of Articles of Gold, Silver & others, **14.** India's share in World's total Jewellery export.

**Speaker:** Jayprakash Bansilal Somani, MBA (Foreign Trade), LL. B. Advocate, Supreme Court of India & IP www.jayprakashsomani.com Call: P. A. 9322188701.

**5. Export Import Finance Management with LC, ECGC & Venture Capital.**

**Description** -You can understand A to Z about International Finance with LC, ECGC & Venture Capital in simple language & with illustrations. 11 videos of this course will create positive spark among you regarding International Finance Management with practical tips. Chance to ask your query to Somani Sir every week.

**Topics : 1.** Export Import Finance Management with LC, ECGC & Venture Capital, **2.** Which is good & excellent source of finance, **3.** Banking Finance, **4.** List of Banks which provides finance for International Business, **5.** How to start business in Less or Zero Capital, **6.** Letter of Credit, **7.** Types of LCs **8.** Scrutiny of L/C, **9.** ECGC Policy, **10.** Venture Capital Finance., **11.** Ideal formula of Investment & continues growth.

**Speaker:** Jayprakash Bansilal Somani, MBA (Foreign Trade), LL. B. Advocate, Supreme Court of India & IP www.jayprakashsomani.com Call: P. A. 9322188701.

**6. Shipping & Logistics in International Business with live links of Ports, ICDs, CHAs etc.**

**Description** - This Course is helpful to any Businessman, Professionals, Entrepreneurs, Exporters, Importers, CHAs, & Students.

Course contains following 10 Videos + Study Material+ PDF Books. Access to this course is for Two Years. Expected duration of this course is three months only.

**Topics : 1.** Shipping & Logistics in International Business with live links of Ports, ICDs, CHAs etc, **2.** Roll of CHA in Shipping & Logistics of International Business, **3.** How to find good & genuine CHA, **4.** Courier/

post service for small parcel, **5.** India's important Ports & ICDs with live links, **6.** How & what to study Ports/ ICDs websites, **7.** Art to reduce charges of Shipping & logistics, **8.** Information about some Top International Ports with live links, **9.** Roll of Customs in Exports & Imports,**10.** How to become CHA .

**Speaker:** Jayprakash Bansilal Somani, MBA (Foreign Trade), LL. B. Advocate, Supreme Court of India & IP www.jayprakashsomani.com Call: P. A. 9322188701.

**7. International Business Marketing Part 1: Finding Potential & Genuine Buyers for Exports and Suppliers for Imports.**

**Description -**You can understand Seven Excellent ways to Find Potential & Genuine Buyers for Exports and Suppliers for Imports with illustrations. 11 videos of this course will create positive spark among you regarding International Business Marketing with practical tips. Chance to ask your query to Somani Sir every week.

**Topics : 1.** International Business Marketing Part 1: Finding Potential & Genuine Buyers for Exports and Suppliers for Imports,**2.** Seven Excellent Ways to find Potential Buyers for Exports, **3.** Top 20 B to B Websites in the World, **4.** Searching Potential Buyers from B to B Sites. Is this safe & good way to search potential buyers, **5.** Searching Potential Buyers through Export Promotional Councils & Its Magazines, **6.** Searching Potential Buyers with help from Embassies, **7.** Searching Potential Buyers through Chamber of Commerce at global level, **8.** Searching Potential Buyers from International Trade Fairs & Exhibitions, **9.** Searching Potential Buyers through your friends & relatives or any Indian Person in focus countries, **10.** How to find focus countries for your products or services, **11.** Taking references from establish buyer/seller.

**Speaker:** Jayprakash Bansilal Somani, MBA (Foreign Trade), LL. B. Advocate, Supreme Court of India & IP www.jayprakashsomani.com Call: P. A. 9322188701.

**8. International Business Marketing Part 2: Communication Skill to take repeated orders from Potential Buyers**

**Description -** You can learn Perfect Communication Skills to initiate International Trade with foreign buyers and art to take repeated orders from these Potential Buyers with illustrations. 11 videos of this course will create positive spark among you to reach upto One Star Exporter Level rapidly and subsequent journey to reach upto Five Star Export House. Chance to ask your query to Somani Sir every week.

**Topics :1.** International Business Marketing Part 2: Communication Skill to take repeated orders from Potential Buyers,**2.** Preparation of Impressive Company Profile, **3.** Excellent Product CatLog for International Market, **4.** Phone Calls with maintaining dignity of ourself & our country, **5.** Sending emails, **6.** Sending what's app messages, **7.** Technique of repeated follow up, **8.** Art of taking 100% advance payments, **9.** Before giving credit facility how to look credibility of potential buyers or suppliers, **10.** Art of earning good profit of margin, **11.** Art of managing international clients.

**Speaker:** Jayprakash Bansilal Somani, MBA (Foreign Trade), LL. B. Advocate, Supreme Court of India & IP www.jayprakashsomani.com Call: P. A. 9322188701.